The Zelensky Method

THE
ZELENSKY
METHOD

GRANT FARRED

Westphalia Press
An Imprint of the Policy Studies Organization
Washington, DC
2022

Westphalia Press
An imprint of Policy Studies Organization
1367 Connecticut Avenue NW
Washington, D.C. 20036
info@ipsonet.org

ISBN: 978-1-63723-823-3

Cover and interior design by Jeffrey Barnes
jbarnesbook.design

Daniel Gutierrez-Sandoval, Executive Director
PSO and Westphalia Press

Updated material and comments on this edition
can be found at the Westphalia Press website:
www.westphaliapress.org

ACKNOWLEDGEMENTS

This essay began with a conversation I had with my friend Tim Campbell. Many of the concepts key to this essay owe a great deal to Tim. I am, as always, grateful to him. My editor, Daniel Gutierrez, made it all seem so simple. I am still not sure how everything happened so quickly and efficiently, but I know that it would have been impossible without Daniel. *Gracias.*

Juanita found a way to make "lyrical" sound pejorative. *Mi amor,* what is there left to say? My friend David Ellison made Dickensian jokes which, unfortunately for me, hit the mark. Finally, writing this book brought into view, unerringly, the three intellectual milieus to which I will always remain indebted.

There are too many folks from these milieus to thank individually, but R.O. Dudley (April 1924–May 2009) and Morgan MacArthur (both LHS), Stan Ridge (UWC; 1942–2018), and Michael Hardt, Fred Jameson, VY Mudimbe, Orin Starn, and Ken Surrin (all Lit Program) deserve a mention.

PREFACE

This essay takes its title from a Stephen Colbert joke. In the wake of Russian president Vladimir Putin's invasion of neighboring Ukraine, Russia was hit with a number of sanctions—most of them economic, mainly involving the isolation of Russia from the global financial system. The decision to deny Russia access to the SWIFT banking system, through which the world conducts most of its financial transactions, was considered especially significant. International pressure was put on global companies doing business in Russia to withdraw. More than four hundred and fifty companies, including H&M, MacDonalds, Nokia, PepsiCo, Starbucks, Apple, Shell, Visa and Mastercard, answered the call.[1] Some of these global corporations pulled out completely, some, such as PepsiCo engaged in a partial withdrawal (continuing to provide "baby food, formula, milk and dairy products"),[2] while others announced their withdrawal but are in effect continuing to do business in Russia. Other corporations, among which number Caterpillar, Citi, Cargill and Hilton remain operative. "Too much exposure" is the logic governing Citi Corp's decision, while Caterpillar's indifference to human suffering, as the 2003 deaths of American Rachel Corrie and Englishman Tom Hurndall in Gaza by an Israeli soldier driving a Caterpillar tractor[3] proved almost twenty years ago, comes as no surprise.[4] There was also a matter which will preoccupy us significantly in the course of this essay—the freezing of the assets by the European Union (EU) and the US of Russian oligarchs sympathetic to Putin. (Oligarchs sometimes go by a more, or, less, I'm not sure, pejorative name: "Kremlingarchs."[5] Has a ring to it, I must admit.) In the 1980s this form of economic sanctions as a means of moral warfare went by the name of "divestment." More targeted, granted, because it was aimed at the white apartheid regime in South Africa, but the overall strategy is eminently recognizable, nonetheless.

One of the 450 companies to pull out of Russia is Netflix, an economic decision which allowed Colbert to follow a different line of attack. The cultural boycott being imposed on Russia, broadly speaking, was Colbert's preferred target. The cultural boycott included, among forms of sanctioning the Putin regime, the non-release of Hollywood movies in Russia, the cancellation of musical events scheduled to take place in Russia, and, most apropos for the purposes of this essay, the shutting down of streaming platforms, thereby denying Russians access to shows they'd grown accustomed to watching.

Colbert's joke turned on Netflix suspending its service to Russia. In its place, Colbert proposed, Russians would now have to depend on a new streaming service, one he dubbed *NYETFLIX*. The name itself is, of course, a double whammy. Not only is there, needless to say, no such streaming service as *NYETFLIX*, but, in Russian, *Nyet* means "No." It follows then, that there will be "No Netflix" on a streaming platform called "No Netflix."

One of the shows Colbert proposed for this nonexistent service was "The Zelensky Method." Colbert was referencing a Netflix series, starring Michael Douglas, called the Kominsky Method." Hence the title of this essay, which can be read (if one were in an ironic frame of mind) as a response to Colbert's call for a show called "The Zelensky Method"—a title which we will subject to a fuller critique shortly.

Colbert's fictitious creation, "The Zelensky Method," is of course an homage to the Ukrainian president Volodymyr Zelensky, himself a TV actor. (Volodymyr Oleksandrovych Zelenskyy; Ukrainian: *Володимир Олександрович Зеленський*; commonly transliterated as "Zelensky.") Zelensky plays Vasily Petrovich Goloborodko, a Ukrainian history teacher in a series called *Servant of the People*— (*Слуга Народу*), a history teacher who, almost through no fault of his own, finds himself elevated to the Ukrainian presidency. It was on *Servant of the People*, during an episode that aired on New Year's Eve 2019, that Zelensky announced his candidacy for the Ukrainian presidency, the pronouncement taking even his wife by surprise. This was a TV show, which ran for three seasons (2015-19, with a movie version coming out in 2016), that brought together art, artifice, and Ukrainian and Russian politics in a heady television cocktail. Funny, by all accounts, and portentous—as if the "revolution" would not only "be live," thereby mangling Gil

Scott-Heron's brash logic, but it would be foretold on TV. (Herron, we remember, promised on his 1974 album, "The revolution will not be televised, the revolution will be live.") *Servant of the People*, broadcast in both Ukraine and Russia, then, probably had more in common with Greek or Shakespearean tragedy than with 1970s spoken-word radicalism.

Art and politics all find their confluence in Zelensky. The Ukrainian president is the actor who played a Ukrainian president who became the Ukrainian president. More than that, Zelensky *is* now the Ukrainian president locked in mortal combat with Russia. "The Zelensky Method" traces for us the transition from artifice— the TV show—to reality. Truth and fiction, fiction and truth, *Servant of the People* becomes president of a people he is sworn to serve. Be careful of what you wish for you when you announce your political ambitions on TV. Be even more careful of who you it is you play on TV because you might very well become that character.

All of these coincidences are just weird, and, as such, impossible to ignore. At the very least, all these coincidences suggest, as if through cultural clairvoyance, that it was art, the TV show, and artifice, creating a character who would become real, which brought the future history of Ukraine to life before it actually occurred. Art comes before life. Art is the future life of the nation. "*Servant of the People:*" a nation's political life foretold.

Our commonsense understanding that fiction cannot hold a candle to actual events—"truth is stranger than fiction"—is inverted— and reversed—in Zelensky's case. *Servant of the People* shows, at least in this case, that fiction enacted a truth to which reality would have to catch up. The Zelensky method is fiction as the truth of history that history has not yet reached. The reversal of the normal order of political logic. In order to become Ukrainian president, one must first play a Ukrainian president on TV. Acting is, or, as, its own prescient truth.

All of which made the name of Colbert's fictional show too good to pass up as a title. Hence, *The Zelensky Method*.

Even as this essay takes its name from and recognizes Volodymyr Zelensky's importance to the struggle that the Ukrainian people are waging against Putin, it also presents Zelensky as a symbolic figure— that is, as a historical actor who finds himself in a situation not in the least of his own making. It must be said that Zelensky has adapted with remarkable poise and courage in this moment of grave national and international crisis. Given that Zelensky's presidency was floundering just months before Putin's decision to invade Ukraine, tainted by scandal and ineffective leadership, he has responded to this existential threat with a brave, determined face. And with the kind of elan that was always beyond, say, the US's Harry Truman. Dropping the A-bomb, measuring up to General Douglas MacArthur's exploits in the Pacific, or devising a plan to rebuild Europe as George Marshall did, producing a Cold War policy as Secretary of State Dean Acheson did, was not within Truman's capabilities. Truman seemed to lack the intellectual vision, the political nous and the personal gravitas of those around him. Truman was thrust into history by FDR's sudden death into a role for which he always appeared ill-suited. But, in one way or another, Truman, recently described as the "ultimate incidental President, a pipsqueak senator from Independence, Missouri,"[6] managed, despite or maybe even because of his limitations. Truman met the occasion. Zelensky has shown himself almost relishing the opportunity to rise to the occasion.

Forget about "pipsqueak senators." Cometh the hour, cometh the comic actor. Zelensky coming to stand as the public face of his nation—Volodymyr Zelensky is both Ukraine's comic actor-turned-first citizen, and President Zelensky, the leader on whom all national and, increasingly, international democratic hopes rest. In the process, the president now stands before us as a figure who is larger than himself, a global representative and incarnation of his people.

And, like all larger-than-life figures, Zelensky's status comes with a proportionate vulnerability. Putin, it is said, has a team of snipers out to get Zelensky. It's as if we are watching, in real time, a spy thriller unfold. There is a very large target on Zelensky's back.

For his part, as I said, Zelensky has warmed to the challenge. Rather than retreating from public view because of how he is being targeted, he has done the opposite. Zelensky has made himself not less, but more, visible—an even bigger target, as if taunting Putin, as if daring the Russian alpha male to do his damnedest. We all know how Putin likes to adopt macho poses for public consumption. But with Zelensky hiding in full public view, is Putin "man enough" to take action against Zelensky? Every time Zelensky steps out in public, he is calling Putin's bluff. So far it seems to be working. The TV comic is showing Putin as nothing but a faux-macho man. One can almost hear, to the horror of the Russian Orthodox Church and its faithful, the strains of the Village People's "Macho, Macho Man" playing in the background.

Putin is no student of history, but he is, at his core, a KGB operative. (Even if he was only a middling, mid-ranking spy; even if he is only a former taxi driver hell bent on eradicating every shred of the mediocrity that is his modest past. Hell hath no fury like a taxi driver scorned; and by a Ukrainian actor, no less.) And as a spy Putin may have done the political calculus—a calculus which he will surely know does not favor him. Alive Zelensky is a threat—beloved by a world enthralled by his courage, a world moved to act against Putin because of Zelensky's rhetorical aptitude. Zelensky seems to know exactly what to say, not only when, but to whom. Zelensky is the darling of democratic liberals, lefties of all stripes. Indeed, Zelensky offers the Western left the chance to embrace a critique of capitalism, especially crony capitalism (those "Kremlingarchs" didn't get so rich by accident), that the European and US left in particular has thus far refused to voice. There is a reflexive reticence on the part of the European left to take to task the kind of monopoly capitalism that has flourished in Russia under Putin; a reticence no doubt borne out of Western leftists' conflation of contemporary Russia, no matter how nostalgically, with the communist project that was the October Revolution. Putin thus gets to have it both ways. Given a pass by Western leftists reluctant to condemn what used to be, with the critical exception that was Stalinism, an ideological ally (even though Putin is no communist nor is he in any way sympathetic to, say, the redistribution of wealth), Putin can rely on leftist reticence in the West while practicing state capture to his heart's content. It is as if the Trinidadian-born Marxist, CLR James, did not provide an ideological critique all those decades ago when he named Stalinist economic policy "state capitalism."

Putin is what happens when Stalinist economic inclination finds itself in a position to exploit technological advancement. Putin is what emerges when the machinations of global capital, every place is less a nation or a community than the opportunity for new markets, new sources of cheap labor, or the production of a new class hungry to participate in consumer society, is left unchecked. Putin is, in this moment, only the most visible but uncritiqued beneficiary of a global left seemingly bereft of a project that can resist the relentless march of "feral capitalism."[7] Putin is what happens when communism, or, socialism, if you prefer, fails in the very place where communism first saw the light of a Marxist day. For the global left, Putin —and all that he has done and all that he would like to do—presents a historic opportunity. One that must not be missed.

No wonder TV cameras the world over can't seem to get enough Volodymyr Zelensky. It has been a long time since so much coalesced in a solitary figure.

Still, there is temporary solace to be found in the fact that Putin is in a bind entirely of his own making.

Alive and denouncing Putin, alive and imploring the world to act against Putin, demanding sanctions, urgently requesting military support, calling for a no-fly zone, Zelensky is Putin's PR nightmare. Zelensky has recruited right to his cause.

A dead Zelensky, however, is an entirely different matter. Martyrs never die. Blaise Compaoré, responsible for the assassination of Burkina Faso's first president, Thomas Sankara, lives in infamy in the Ivory Coast.[8] For his part, the revolutionary Thomas Sankara endures. The Congo's first leader, Patrice Lumumba, is the stuff of legend, made into an icon by a Raoul Peck film (which very much has the feel of a documentary with hagiographic overtones), titled, of course, "Lumumba." Lumumba's Belgian-backed antagonist,[9] Moïse-Kapenda Tshombe, who declared himself president of the mineral-rich Katanga province, has been forgotten, at best condemned to history as a failed businessman and a grubby and expedient political opportunist. Twice exiled to Spain by the government that replaced Lumumba, Tshombe died, unmourned, in Algiers.

For his courage and his fortitude, for his facility with the global language of democracy, no matter that we may differ as to the meaning of "democracy," for his determination to secure the future of his people and to bring peace to them, and to Russia too, even if it's not (the) peace exactly that Putin wants, Zelensky is surely a shoo-in for the 2022 Nobel Peace Prize, should Zelensky still be alive come October. With a little tweak, Ukraine's resistance to Putin's predations could easily be the stuff of a Tom Clancy thriller—*Hunt until Red October.*

An assassinated Zelensky or a Zelensky killed in battle is surely not a prospect Putin wants to countenance. Let us not even contemplate the catastrophic effects that would follow an attack on Zelensky caught on camera. It could inspire, as the death of martyrs and national/international heroes is apt to do, generations of Ukrainians to commit themselves to the liberation of their people. We can only imagine how it might inform the aspirations of any Ukrainian generation, present and future, who find themselves in opposition to Russia, to say nothing of how it might rally other nations opposed to Russia.[10]

Surely Putin is politically calculating enough not to "canonize" Volodymyr Zelensky—canonization being a term used ironically for the Jewish Zelensky? This, however, is Putin. Who knows what he might do? Does Putin even know what he is capable of? All things considered, it is probably best to never say never with Putin. Or, never say *Nyet,* as the case might be. To never say *Nyet* to the prospect of a nuclear attack on Ukraine.

In order not to fall into the trap that Putin has set for himself, *The Zelensky Method,* much as it admires Zelensky, at once proceeds through a historically grounded interest in him while also seeking to lift Zelensky, to coin a phrase, out of himself. That is, this essay tries to understand both what Zelensky says and does, and how he says and does it. There is, however, a complementary aspect to the Zelensky effect, an aspect that requires us to acknowledge that in crucial ways in which Zelensky exceeds himself. In short, the political actor who has emerged into public view since February 24th, 2022, is as much a media-political construct as he is a political leader doing everything possible to avert the destruction of his country. And if we learned nothing else from, say, US imperialist adventurism in Vietnam or the ignominious Soviet defeat in Afghanistan, we surely learned one thing. A nation rallying to defend itself will always, no matter the human and economic cost, regardless of the time it takes, put paid to the empire.

However, even as this essay recognizes what it is Zelensky is trying to do, *The Zelensky Method* has no illusions about Zelensky. He is, like all historical figures, an imperfect actor thrust into a situation not of his own making. And if any proof of Zelensky's political flaws were needed, there are the revelations contained in the Pandora Papers about possible corrupt business deals, kickbacks to cronies, and the like. The revelations about Zelensky in the Pandora Papers show him to be as politically fallible as any elected representative—as a politician who benefited from shady business deals. Furthermore, as we already noted, Zelensky was hardly a sparkling economic or political success in the brief period between his April, 2019 electoral triumph over Petro Poroshenko, and Putin's invasion. As recently as late-January, 2022, Zelensky publicly cast doubt on Washington's warnings about a Russian invasion.

Nevertheless, Zelensky is a figure made by the history of the present, who represents a set of political values. He may even speak to a public desire to find in an elected representative that rarest of qualities, morality, the sense that he is a political figure trying to do the right thing. To do so, Zelensky has come embody a casual military bearing that does not seem to be militaristic—at least not militaristic for its own sake. Zelensky's casual, incidental "militariness," occupying the role of reluctant but determined commander-in-chief, is evident to us in his by now much-hyped sartorial self-presentation. No fancy military uniform, no starched military jacket emblazoned with medals—think Idi Amin. In its place, Zelensky prefers bare-bones camo outfits, cargo military pants topped always by what is fast becoming his signature clothing item, that military green T-shirt. There are occasional public moments when, whether for personal safety or show is not clear, he will don a flak jacket. Worn over that green T-shirt, it serves only to enhance his reluctant militarism.

A great deal of Zelensky's effective self-presentation derives, then, from his mode of address. But there is more to it. Zelensky always seems to speak frankly, outlining the situation in the most basic language. No florid rhetorical touches, no poetic metaphors. Importantly, Zelensky always seems to speak directly not only to the camera, but all individual viewers. He is speaking to you, to me, never to *us*. Every member of his audience is an individual worthy of individual address. His speaking is fortified by the way in which he gives voice to a set of democratic expectations. Democratic expectations that have a global resonance. Zelensky coordinates a greater international solidarity. Through this coordination, Zelensky brings into view not only Europe, and the grave threat that it might yet face, but the world. Zelensky reminds the Finns of their historic struggle against Russian aggression during the 1939 "Winter War" in which Russia, despite its supposed military superiority, was forced into signing a peace treaty after some three months of combat. Zelensky calls on the South Koreans to conjure up memories of their own 1950-53 struggle against the North, in which they were able to secure their state with assistance from the US and the United Nations (UN).[11] Now, Zelensky, implores South Koreans, is the time to honor that memory by dispatching heavy weapons to Ukraine in order to ensure his state's survival. In addressing South Korea in this way, Zelensky's making of the Ukrainian resistance a matter of shared global concern sheds light on the failure of other countries such as India[12] and South Africa to live up to the promises of their anti-colonial and anti-apartheid pasts, respectively.

Zelensky has made Ukraine a litmus test on global democracy. The choice is simple, as longtime Putin antagonist, and Russia's most indefatigable opposition leader, Alexei Navalny, reminds us. The choice is not between good and evil. That matter is settled. What is at stake, rather, what position you take in the battle between evil and neutrality. Consciously or not, Zelensky has picked up the Navalny mantle and, in so doing, Zelensky is playing the president he played in *Servant of the People* to perfection—so much so that, in the process of executing his role to perfection, is Zelensky not, to phrase the matter in the colloquial, also *playing* Putin to perfection?

While Putin may see himself as being in control, the relative ineffectiveness of the Russian military suggests he is not in control; the KGB operative turned puppet master of the Russian people is confronting a dilemma. After all, every time Zelensky opens his mouth, whether to TV crews in Kyiv or when he is addressing august bodies of politicians gathered to hear him, Putin is at a disadvantage.

The world believes Zelensky.

In his turn, Putin is left to bemoan the rise of "Russophobia." The surest sign of Putin's pathos is to be found, for example, in his railing against Italian universities who considered cancelling a class on Dostoevsky to register their opposition to Russia's violence against Ukraine. A decision, mercifully, reversed. *Crime and Punishment* will be studied. Dostoevsky can rest easy, for now.

Still and all, it's as though Zelensky and Putin are caught in a game, playing by a set of rules that follows the lines of inquiry posed by the early 1980s pop song: "Now tell me who,/who's fooling who?/are you fooling me?/or am I fooling you?" (A very catchy song by the group "One Way." It may have been their only hit but it was, in my recollection, oh-so danceable.) Is Zelensky even trying to "fool" Putin, or is Putin already doing a good enough job of "fooling" himself? Putin certainly does not seem to have a firm grip on the military situation in Ukraine. What kind of mind, we wonder, does it take to make Putin and Russia the victims in this war against Ukraine? Putin is only a victim if we attribute at least a smidgeon of political substance—and there is no reason we should, but let's suspend disbelief for a second—to his insistence that he and Russia are the victims of a grand global conspiracy led by a Jewish Ukrainian Nazi and a West intolerant of Russian culture.

And, in our social media world, that leaves Putin with only one option: grasping at straws.

In his desperation, Putin is left to declaim "cancel culture." And his analogy rests, precipitously, on one that depends on the fallacious logic that there is a similarity between the backlash against Russia for its invasion of Ukraine and the attacks JK Rowling received for her critique of trans culture. Of all the gin joints, to mix metaphors, that's the hill on which Putin chooses to die? Seriously? JK Rowling, swiftly, distanced herself from Putin.

What's a czar to do when even a fellow-victim of cancel culture refuses his entreaties?

On the other hand, there is something entirely foolish, silly, even, when a powerful leader declares war on a neighboring state and suggests that he and his people are being wronged. On second thought, its neither silly nor foolish. It is simply offensive to all the dead.

There is indeed a form of cancel culture at work. It is Putin attacking and killing his neighbors and committing war crimes in the process. That is indeed an act of cancellation. The permanent cancellation of life, of tens of thousands of Ukrainian lives.

Here, cancel culture is the determination to cancel an entire (people and their) culture. Offensive, as I said. And that's a lot different from being foolish.

It is something akin to what Karl Marx defined as false consciousness. False consciousness as the willful belief in something that is patently untrue—pretending to believe a lie. A significant number of Russians, for a variety of reasons, none of them justifiable, are showing themselves willing to believe a lie. At best, they have submitted to what two German refugees from Nazism, Theodor Adorno and Max Horkheimer, propose as a form of myth. For Adorno and Horkheimer, false clarity, as in Putin's repeated assertion that the Ukrainian people are under the sway of Nazis, is a form of myth.

Myth-making, especially when it is works in the cause of imperial violence, is at least as dangerous as false consciousness. False clarity can be fatal, and not only to the other. The (Russian) self too is at risk. If not immediately, then surely in the aftermath of the violence committed in the name of the myth.

There's a difference, a difference that the myth cannot overcome, between cancel culture, social media-style, and relentlessly bombing your neighbors because they won't give credence to your untruths. It's the kind of difference, one hopes, that comes with a signpost—a signpost that reads, "This is a War Crime. Next stop, for the perpetrator, The Hague."

An ominous warning. One doubts that it will be heeded. After all, the myth is both a resilient and a many-headed creature.

LIFTING ZELENSKY OUT OF HIMSELF

By lifting Zelensky out of himself, it becomes possible to see what he is doing, and to see how he is doing it. Lifting Zelensky out of himself also, however, makes it necessary to provide a reflection on the effect of what it is Zelensky is doing and how it is he is doing it. Lifting Zelensky out of himself is an attempt to understand what is being called here the "Zelensky Method." It is to consider this method, to locate Zelensky in his method while also recognizing that there are likely moments in which man and method converge—converge into singularity. And to acknowledge that there are also those moments when method triumphs over man. And, vice versa, when man has the upper hand over method.

Of course, written as it is in the very moment in which history is unfolding, *The Zelensky Method* is by no means, nor can it be, a complete project. This essay has no pretense to being definitive. In truth, however, no writing or thinking can ever be complete or definitive, no matter that it might pretend otherwise. Still, writing as events appear to be and are changing, literally from one minute to the next, is a response to the urgency of the moment that carries in it a particular danger. It is a danger that cannot be avoided and must be acknowledged. However, to be in the world in such a moment as the Russian invasion of Ukraine depends on many responses, and not all of those responses promise to be equally effective. In the larger scheme of things, a critique of Zelensky is a dubious undertaking. And yet, it may be that what is most necessary now is to think how it is Volodymyr Zelensky is going about the business of securing a future, a peaceful future, we hope but have no guarantee of, for Ukraine.

Phrased differently—*The Zelensky Method* is a provisional study of a president's method of acting in the face of an existential threat to his people. Or, by what method can authenticity, a key concept in this essay, counteract (the) myth?

The Zelensky Method studies the method of an actor who is not a method actor.

Nevertheless, this essay strives to achieve a presentation of Zelensky, a presentation that accounts for the Ukrainian president as both symbol and actual figure of our historical present. Zelensky as making history even as he is being made by history. Or, we might wonder, was Zelensky simply not made *for* history?

And, to do this we must, as has been acknowledged, lift Zelensky out of himself without ever untethering him from the moment in which he finds himself—a moment as much thrust upon him as a moment to which he gives shape and content. Still, this essay offers no panoramic view of Zelensky. It does not aspire to transcend. Instead, this essay explores what Zelensky is doing and the complications, inadequacies, achievements and shortcomings that attend as much to his actions as to his self-presentation. *The Zelensky Method* is then but one of the many first words about Zelensky. We are, simultaneously, too far and too near from the final word on him.

And that is a recognition written in fear.

By lifting Zelensky out of himself, by making his thinking present to us, the unspoken—now spoken—hope of *The Zelensky Method* is that those fears will come to nothing. That Ukraine will survive, and, in so doing, will compel all of us to reflect on how it is we want to be in the world.

Much of the spirit that is writing desperately for a future that will displace our historical present, without leaving the past to itself, unthought, fuels this essay. *The Zelensky Method* constitutes a writing for, but not in the name of, the survival of a people. What matters above all is harnessing the work of political imagination to the cause of proposing, and in so doing establishing, a new set of human relations—a writing fueled, of course, by a sense of urgency, a sense of urgency that derives directly from the perils Ukraine faces.

And this urgency manifests itself often in the most obvious acknowledgement. On more than a few occasions, *The Zelensky Method* announces itself as provisional. It states: "at the time of writing." Not a statement but a provisional description. As in: "at the time of writing, March 25th, 2022, Ukrainian forces are launching a count-er-offensive against Russian troops in the Kyiv suburbs. With some success."[13] This has the provisional benefit of being accurate. But, as with all that is provisional, the tide could turn, and Russians could retake the suburb. As such, we should admit that there is always in the provisional both hope and fear—the hope that things will turn out the way in which we would like them to, and the fear that things could go awry. More obviously, the provisional acknowledges that it is a writing against time. The provisional understands that whatever claims it makes, whatever description of events it offers, things could quickly change, making those claims obsolete and those descriptions inaccurate. In this way, for example, "three Russians killed" at the time of writing can quickly become, say, five or eight. Nevertheless, subject to change as the provisional is, it is also a commitment to an argument, a dedicated critique that seeks to intervene even as the situation in question remains fluid and ever-changing.

It may very well be the recognition that it is writing against time that gives the provisional its special quality in relation to writing. The provisional makes us grasp writing itself as though it were already not only a necessary act, but that writing is itself a declaration of belief in what must be—a tentative testament to what might be, as though what must be can only emerge out of writing. Knowing that every writing is not only provisional, but constitutively incomplete. Every writing acknowledges, instinctively, that it leaves several things unsaid. It is thus that the provisional takes its solace. What is more, the provisional proceeds to find succor in solace, insisting that no writing or thinking is ever complete. It is merely abandoned, to be revisited at some unknow future date.

Now "who's fooling who?" Am I fooling me?

KEY CONCEPTS

To understand Zelensky's presentation of himself and of the Ukrainian people, *The Zelensky Method* relies at crucial moments on two inter-related concepts: authenticity and common sense. Zelensky's ability to, as of this moment, continue to rally the Ukrainian people and to unite the world against Russia derives from his ability to, in the vernacular, "keep it real." Simply put, when Zelensky speaks, his audience believes him. Zelensky is able to relate to his audience. In its turn, his audience demonstrates faith in him. Zelensky's audience trusts what he is saying. And his audiences, as we know, include everything from national representative bodies (parliaments, and so on) to television audiences to those who watch him on social media sites.

The audience trusts Zelensky because he speaks in what is can broadly be understood as common sense. What he says makes sense. What he says seems to express exactly not only how things are, but, indeed, how they should be. This is not to say that Zelensky is without his own inauthenticity. After all, the Pandora Papers, misjudging Putin, put any such illusions to rest. (In fairness to Zelensky, many other world leaders and international organizations were similarly guilty.)

However, *The Zelensky Method* recognizes that, in presenting Zelensky as an "authentic revolutionary," his historic shortcomings do not matter quite so much—if, indeed, they matter at all. What matters is Zelensky's is his ability to speak directly, effectively, and with a profound sense of honesty about not only the way things are in Ukraine because of Russia's constant bombardment, but about the ways in which the world should do everything it can to put an end to Putin's violence. Zelensky offers us a vision of how things should be in Ukraine, how they should be in Belarus, and how they should be in Russia. As the world increasingly recognizes the depth of support for Putin's adventurism, we are witnessing a shift—not yet decisive, but incipient—in designation. (While this is still, at the time of writing, "Putin's war," it might not be very long before we know it as "Russia's war." A case of sometime countries get the leaders who represent their worst tendencies.)

As we know, Belarus' president Alexander Lukashenko is a close Putin ally. Having ruled for 28 years, Lukashenko has quashed the Belarussian opposition. As a result of this, there is a large Belarussian diaspora not only in Lithuania and Poland, but also in Ukraine. Several of these Belarussian dissidents have taken up arms for Ukraine,[14] even as the Belarus itself has become a staging ground for Russian forces. Belarussians are fighting Russia in the hope that a Ukrainian victory will make it possible to rid Belarus of Lukashenko. How things might be, then, as a movement with offshoots far beyond Kyiv and Dnipro. Zelensky, Ukrainians, Belarussians, each fashioning themselves according to their own conception of what it means to be a "Servant of the People." Sometimes those national self-fashionings overlap, coincide with, and reinforce each other. At other times each must follow its own trajectory. Still, in each struggle there is the hope that a victory for one will, in time, be a victory for all. Out of one, many.

This thread, the figure—the motif—of the "Servant of the People," runs through and animates this essay. Again, authenticity is understood here in its common sense articulation and is key because Zelensky is practiced in the art—already a slippage between the performative and "keeping it real" —of what it takes to address his audience in such a way as to make them believe him. Of course, this motif invites a comparison. If Zelensky is not only the self-styled "Servant of the People," then, by way of contrast, Putin is cast as the czar intent upon making the people serve him. That is the imperial way. The Russian people are born to, well, "serf." (A role, as I just said, that many Russians seem happy to play.) The Russian people made, and not without their own submission to false consciousness or myth-making, to "serf" an imperial leader—an imperial leader accountable to no one but himself. Why ever would Russians want to return to the status of "serfs" when their neighbors are inspired to heroic heights by their very own "Servant?"

The Zelensky Method also takes aim at a range of actors, both international and (Russian) national. The international actors range from Israel to South Africa, from Brazil[15] to India[16]—nations that have decided that self-interest, in whatever guise it assumes and no matter that it seeks to misrepresent itself in the soul-destroying language that by bureaucratic-speak (the very opposite of Zelensky's authentic common sense), takes precedence over thousands of dead Ukrainians.

The critique of the Russian oligarchs, oligarchs made rich with the Kremlin's support (state-capture can be said to be a competitive national sport in Russia), informs much of the essay. The focus of the critique of the oligarchs, however, is trained on sport. Specifically, on the Russian oligarch Roman Abramovich and the English Premier League club Abramovich owned until the war began, Chelsea Football Club (FC). Sport and culture have been key to purchasing respectability for Putin's oligarchs—not in Russia so much as in European capitals and in American cultural centers from New York to Hollywood.

RE-CREATING EUROPE, AND BEYOND

Zelensky, in his address to Europe, is not only speaking to its leaders. He is also addressing its people. Directly. In this post-Brexit moment, with a Europe fractured in part because of the rise of strong men in countries such as Hungary and Poland, with Marie le Pen playing footsie with Putin and promising to soft peddle on him should she defeat Emmanuel Macron and ascend to the French presidency in 2022, Zelensky is appealing not to individual nations but to Europe, a post-Brexit political entity that he is creating anew. Zelensky's Europe can be said to be an imaginary version in which Europe now begins in Crimea.

However, it is not only Europe that Zelensky has made ready for re-creation. Zelensky's arrival on the world stage stands as an invitation for the entire democratic world to stand in solidarity with each other. "Democratic" here means those nations in the world that not only proclaim themselves to be democratic but have in place structures accountable to the democratic process—regular election cycles, an independent judiciary, the right of *habeas corpus*, and equality before the law, among other aspects of daily political life. To stand in solidarity, in the moment of record, with each other—with each other against tyrannical forces. A standard of democratic allegiance by which Brazil, China, India, Israel, and South Africa are found wanting.

AND THIS IS HOW THE END BEGAN

Mark this. On February 25th, 2022, the day after he declared war on Ukraine, the Russian president Vladimir Putin's reign ended. Or, as the Chinese painter Huang Rui put it after completing his artwork, a Ukrainian flag with a black/gray circle in the middle augmented by a red stripe running north-south above and below the circle, "Ukraine has already won."[17] Still, an ominous sign, Rui's red line, as though it were the premonition of a divided, east-west, Ukraine—a dividing line well known to Europe, especially in Germany.

At the time of writing, April 20th, 2022 (Hitler's birthday), war still rages in Ukraine. Or, rather, a new war rages in Ukraine. In mid-April, 2022, Russian forces largely withdrew from western Ukraine only to amass along the country's eastern border, and are currently launching a full-scale assault to claim—at least—the Donbas region, home to a significant Russian-speaking population. On April 19th, 2022, Russian Foreign Minister Sergei Lavrov declared, "Another phase of this operation is starting now."[18] There is every reason to expect that this next "phase" is in preparation for a full-fledged attack on eastern Ukraine, thus cleaving Ukraine as we know it in two. No matter. Vladimir Putin is done—done in by Zelensky.

Putin's reign ended with words defiant and noble, but above all, memorable. Rather, they are made memorable by their defiance and nobility—words gilded by their refusal to bow to Putin's un-provoked attack on Ukraine, whose authenticity derive as well from their rejection of U.S. strategic advice. We know these words well. We know them so well that they almost instantly became a meme, a meme made for our age—a meme that would seem to be the off-spring of a self-negating TikTok-Uber hookup. An alimentary political statement: "I don't need a ride. I need ammunition."

All this we glean from that first, short, declarative statement—a statement that is startling, almost bracingly so, and not only for its brevity. It is colloquial. "I don't need a ride" is the kind of thing a friend might say to another, on the order of a polite, "Thanks but no thanks." It is casual in its construction, in its word choice, a turn of phrase one could as easily address to a friend as to a stranger. It is the kind of polite "No, thank you" that is almost guaranteed to be accompanied by a smile. As though one frat boy were saying to another, with no forethought, "I'm good, bro." It is certainly not a sentiment that is expressed with or in anger. One could easily imagine a run-of-the-mill exchange that goes, "I don't need a ride. I've got an Uber coming." A long, long way from "I don't need a ride, the Russian artillery is on its way."

The "Zelensky Method."

It's how you talk with your friends. In familiar terms. No elaborate sentence structure. An everyday vocabulary. No "big words."

Nothing needs to be repeated. Every word, every intention, is born by everyday language so that everybody understands everybody else. Without explication. What is said is what is meant. What is meant is said in such a way that only one meaning can be derived. A simple, shared language.

The "Zelensky Method" leaves the speaker no choice but to practice direct address. And direct address can only be effective when the message is clear, the request is unambiguous, and everybody knows what everybody else means. Clarity. True, not false, clarity. Simple sentences. Everyday language. Language made politically usable. Everyone within earshot, as it were, of Zelensky, must be able to relate to him and to his struggle. It begins with Zelensky, of course, because he must relate to everyone. Zelensky, trained actor that he is, has made a point of knowing his audience. As the actor who played an unwilling president who now finds himself a president, he is adept in the art of address. He has a very good idea of what it takes to reach—to teach—his audience.

In relation to his fellow-Ukrainians, he has executed this task splendidly. No one, Putin least of all, would have expected that he could rally his nation so.

Romantic words, powerful, evocative in their simplicity, spoken by the Ukrainian president facing a fearsome Russian onslaught. "I don't need a ride."

There is general agreement that Putin's "special military operation" in Ukraine has been a surprisingly inept undertaking. At the
time of writing, more than four weeks into the war, the Ukrainians
are holding their own, dogged and determined in their opposition
to Russian forces. Russian forces, meanwhile, are bent on executing Putin's ethno-nationalist war in Ukraine. "Russia," in Putin's ethno-nationalist logic, is not a geo-political unit defined by sovereign
national borders. Putin's "Russia," defined by, as is common to all
ethno-nationalist projects, language, culture, and blood—the last of
which, *Blut und Boden* ("blood and soil"), is a chilling term with an
ugly fascist history. *Blut und Boden* was the basis of the Nazi belief in
Lebensraum, the idea Germany should expand eastward to incorpo-
rate into itself those German-speaking populations. In the logic of
Lebensraum, Germans—or, German-speakers, at least, "ethno-Ger-
mans"—would displace the Slavic and Baltic peoples living there.
Lebensraum is the basis on which Nazi Germany invaded the Sudetenland, a German-speaking area on the border with what was then
Czechoslovakia. Ethno-nationalism should give all cause for pause, a
pause that must begin today with the situation in the Donbas region
of Ukraine.

That is because wherever there are, to Putin's mind, Russian
speakers, people who consider themselves culturally Russian, those
who can trace their lineage, in one way or another, to Russia, all these
people must be brought into the ethno-nationalist fold that is "Russia." The terms of Putin's ethno-nationalism are such that it deems
"defending" "Russians" in Georgia, South Ossetia, and Abkhazia,
"Russian Republics" seized by Putin in 2008, and now Ukraine a
legitimate military action. (However, in contrast to the "special military operation" in Ukraine, Putin's Georgian action lasted less than
two weeks. Russia's annexation of Crimea was all the Ukrainians
were going to allow.) In this regard, Putin is a man of his *Blut und
Boden* word. Interviewed for twenty hours by US film maker Oliver
Stone (2015-17),[19] Putin made clear that the two conditions under
which he would go to war: if either Georgia or Ukraine made over-

tures to NATO. Putin has kept his word. It remains only now for the bill to come due.

Putin may not be much of a reader, but he is a past (KGB) master of Orwellian-speak. "Special military operation," indeed. Above all, an especially inept "special military operation." Russia's military forces appear to lack the preparedness to fight a Ukrainian people determined to defend their national sovereignty. Russian tanks are running out of gas, stuck on the highway to Kyiv. Low on morale, Russian soldiers are said to be quitting; or, not putting up much of a fight and surrendering to the Ukrainians.

Putin's invasion has made our spelling sensitive to the Ukrainian tongue. It is "Kyiv," no longer "Kiev (the Russian spelling of the Ukrainian capital)a name now at the tip of the much of the world's tongue, as are "Lyiv," "Kharkiv," and "Maripuol." Courtesy of Putin, the world is now being given an instant geography lesson in the geopolitics of Eastern Europe. Once more "Crimea" rushes back into the world's political imaginary. *War and Peace* all over again. Crimea, the scene of the original Russian crime. The world fears that this crime, against first the citizens of southeastern Ukraine and now against the very existence of Ukraine itself, will not end in Kyiv or Lyiv.

Suddenly it matters that the world can distinguish between eastern and western Ukraine. Eastern Ukraine, bordered entirely by Russia, has long been targeted for Russian incursion by Putin. It began, as we all know—or, at least, we know a little—about the "breakaway republics" of Donbas and Donetsk. These "republics" lie on the opposite side of the country, far from the capital Kyiv. Since the war began western Ukraine has been made known to the world as Ukrainian refugees, in their hundreds of thousands, flood into Moldova, Romania, Poland, before some of them are offered refuge in places as far away as Ireland, Canada, and the U.S. At the time of writing, Hungary and Slovakia appear to have been spared such an influx, but for how long?[20] Ukrainians are fleeing, as far away from Ukraine as they can get.

Refugees making their way from Ukraine to various places in western Europe are telling tales of beleaguered, maybe even demoralized and at least some of them unmotivated, Russian soldiers. More than a few of these Russian soldiers are deserting rather than fighting this war against their neighbors; and, in some cases, blood relatives, such are the familial links between the two nations. Russian soldiers are roaming Ukrainian streets, finding themselves scolded by elderly Ukrainians. In one case, newly arrived in Italy, after a 22-hour bus ride from Poland, a Ukrainian refugee relates the story of Russian soldiers knocking at their doors in western Ukraine, asking for bread. If it wasn't so violently tragic, so tragically violent, one could almost make a Dickensian joke. "Please, ma'am, can I have a slice?" Or, a French Revolutionary one: "Let them eat Ukrainian cake," a septuagenarian mocks the invaders—if they can find any.

Russian generals, at least six to date, have been killed in combat. Major Generals Andrei Kolesnikov (Kharkiv), Andrei Sukhovetsky (Kharkiv). and Vitaly Gerasimov Kharkiv), all in the first 15 days of fighting. (That number has since increased to either eight or nine, along with 34 colonels.)[21] Six is more generals than Russia lost when it propped up the Syrian regime of Bashir al-Assad.[22] Since then, at least two or possibly three more have been killed:[23] Major General Mityaev (Mariupol), Commander Andrei Modvichev (Kherson), and Lieutenant General Yakov Rezantsev (Kherson), the highest-ranking Russian officer to be killed in the war according to Ukraine's Defense Ministry.

The Russian advance westward in Ukraine is bogged down by not only by fierce Ukrainian defense, but by strategic blunders, low morale, and the lack of technological support. To this we could add a Napoleonic irony. The French general met his end at Waterloo through his foolhardy determination to go east, in the heart of winter, a lesson not learned by a certain German Führer, although Herr Hitler had had almost a century to absorb that lesson. Putin, on the other hand, seems intent on reversing the direction by heading west. In so doing, Putin is tempting fate to make of himself an unfortunate historical aberration. Will Napoleon and Hitler's "Eastern Front" now be joined by Putin's "Western Front?"

This brutal determination to move toward the Polish border, where Ukraine ends, and where a potential world-altering confrontation with NATO, fully backed by the U.S., may ensue. Putin's is a mindset so antithetical to the very imperial American logic he says he opposes. In terms of Manifest Destiny, the American injunction is always to head west, to head for a frontier beyond one's geographical imaginings. Now, in place of that injunction, "Go West," which led to a genocidal onslaught against America's indigenous population, one is tempted to advise Putin, "Don't Go West, 69-year-old man, Don't Go West." Everything is roiling on the Western Front. Will Poland be Putin's Waterloo? Mischievously, however, one would almost prefer that Putin meet his demise in Romania, the self-proclaimed "island of Latinity in a Slavic Sea." Wouldn't that be just so much more fitting? Like his historical forbears, Napoleon and Hitler, Putin would be forced to confront his demise in a land where he has no mastery of the native tongue. Latinity's revenge. A belligerent Slav isolated—drowning? engulfed?—in a sea of an antipathetic Orthodoxy.

ORTHODOX RUSSIAN FASCISM

Or, perhaps, a belligerent former KGB officer who has now adopted, strategically (Putin is by no means a man of faith), wholesale the teachings of (Russian) Orthodox Christian fascism, a strain that has for centuries run through Russian Orthodoxy. From time to time this violent Orthodoxy surfaces, each time as a distinct variant, like a virus seeking ever more fecund ground, as in the teachings of Ivan Ilyin (1883-1954), a philosopher who studied Hegel but also advocated an openly fascist, militarist brand of Orthodoxy. A critic of the October Revolution, Ilyin, who died in Switzerland, regarded communism as sign of the national weakness of the Russian people. (Putin, too, is no communist, although he routinely appeals rhetorically to those of the communist persuasion. Like any half decent politician, Putin is an unabashed opportunist. Every constituency is there for the taking.)

A champion of human inequality (the state is composed of individuals who are inherently unequal to each other), Ilyin, like Putin, regarded any Ukrainian claim to sovereignty as not only unacceptable, but traitorous to Russia—a crime punishable by death, we might imagine. In Ilyin's ideal Russian state, neither totalitarian nor formally democratic (Ilyin was impatient with the franchise and other such trappings of democracy), none are so unequal—to the Russians—as the Ukrainians. At least, so we are free to speculate. Ukrainians: nothing but children of a lesser Orthodox god, hewers of Karelia and Komi wood, drawers of the Volga's water.

More recently, Putin has acquired his own philosopher, the ultranationalist Aleksandr Dugin. A known admirer of Nazism and a Stalinist to boot, Dugin is a fierce critic of what he considers Western hegemony. A self-described conservative, he touts family values that resonate with significant sectors of the U.S.' Republican Party, and Dugin echoes the kind of right-wing ideology that fuels Fox News. Dugin's philosophy turns on unquestioning patriotism, the nuclear family, and a firm belief in Orthodox Christianity, ordered by a strong state. Putin's philosopher disdains any claim to universal human rights. He has no time for what he denigrates as Western individualism. Democracy, for him, is nothing but a Western imposition that should have no place in the reactionary Russian universe of his imagination.

Such are Putin's articles of faith.

Still, with all this, there is a stringency, even an antiseptic dullness, that lingers in the halls of Putin's palace, at least on the surface, and perhaps even a little below that. Putin's palace, tightly controlled it is, could do with a mad romantic figure on the order of Czar Nicolai II's Grigori Rasputin, the Siberian-born *muzhik* (peasant), just to make it a tad more interesting. Rasputin, who as a teenager underwent a religious conversion of Damascus proportions, is credited with saving the Czar and his hemophiliac son, Alexei. This minor miracle made him a court favorite, to the infuriation of the Russian nobles wary of being displaced in the graces of the Romanovs, the Czarina Alexandra in particular. Nor was the Orthodox establishment best pleased with the *muzhik's* inexplicable rise. Rasputin's fellow-peasants were hardly won over either, probably shocked to see *muzhik* flying so preternaturally high. This was, after all, feudal Russia, where everyone was expected to know their place.

The nobles, two of whom eventually murdered him, detested Rasputin because they feared his influence on the Romanovs. The church could not abide him because of the unorthodoxy of his religious practices, unbearable even to an Orthodoxy steeped in the mystical. And the peasants, apparently, were appalled, permanently befuddled by how Rasputin had come to be, well, Rasputin. It is said that they took no pleasure in witnessing the rise to such power by one of their one. And there was, finally, the palace intrigue that swirled around him, not the least of which was the suspicion that he was the Czarina's lover.

On that score, at least, Putin should be sympathetic to Rasputin, given his own amorousness. All those Putin affairs, all those not-so secret daughters. Putin's palace may be dull on the surface, but it is not exactly immune to sexual peccadilloes. In every Russian czar since the ill-fated reign of Nicolai II, there has been a a little Rasputin. And, as we know, Putin's the first Czar since Nicolai II met his historic fate. Dare one hope that history will repeat itself, this time neither as farce nor tragedy but as something on the order of justice? For now, we'll have to make do with Putin's capacity for Rasputin-like mischief of the bedroom variety. In the absence of larger structural changes, the prurient—the pulp and detritus of social media, the kind of nonsense that gets Kanye kicked off social media or the untruths that Donald Trump is known to spout—will have to suffice.

"I DON'T NEED A RIDE. I NEED AMMUNITION."

A simple sentence, Zelensky's, repeated countless times since it first utterance. A simple declarative sentence. Zelensky's is a one-of-a-kind of sentence. It is a sentence global in its effect and empathy-inducing in its resonance. It is Churchillian heroism distilled to two phrases piercing in their clarity. (We'll get to the Churchill in Zelensky shortly.) Zelensky's is the kind of sentence that gives-courage-to-all-in-the-nation-under-attack and has the rest of the democratic world hungering for such a leadership crafted out of political doggerel.

The effect of Zelensky's word, coupled with Russian military incompetence, is undoubted. The Ukrainian president inspired his people with his bravery. In a nation literally under fire, he refused the U.S.'s invitation to evacuate him and his family to safety. He acknowledged himself and his family as, in his understated but dramatic phrasing, as a man and his loved ones made public enemy numbers 1 and 2 by Putin. Instead of seeking safety in a foreign country, which would have meant abandoning his people to their fate—a brutal one, without question—Zelensky chose to remain. Is there method at all in such a political act? Is it not sheer madness? Is madness nothing but the first inklings of a new way of doing things? Out of the madness of "I don't need a ride" emerges a previously unthinkable method.

Zelensky chose to face the danger. An act of madness, surely. He chose to become the most visible part of Ukrainian resistance—the exemplary One who would risk his life for the (Ukrainian) All. To everyone's surprise, Ukraine coalesced around him. To everyone's surprise except the Ukrainians, or so it would seem in retrospect. The Ukrainians gathered themselves, determined to resist Russia's attack on their sovereignty. The annexation of Crimea by Russia must have sorely wounded the Ukrainian people's sense of self—wounded them more deeply than they may have been willing to admit. *Bilse ni. No mas.* Here they would take their stand. Is this the flip side, the upside, if you will, of ethno-nationalism? It rallies the nation in the name of democracy, national sovereignty, and freedom?

Zelensky on the streets of a Kyiv under attack stands, of course, is a sharp contrast to germophobic Putin, sequestered in splendid isolation. His advisers dare not come any closer than the length of his impressive table—30 feet long, it is reputed to be. His confidantes must, similarly, keep their distance lest they infect him with the Covid-19 virus. Whether it be Omicron strain, or some other strain, perhaps the "Omicron II" that is now on the loose in China, matters not to Putin. "Get thee thirty feet away from me," is Putin's nod to Shakespeare's Hamlet. Putin lives, works, and makes decisions, it would seem, safely distanced from everyone. Even when Putin did that rare thing, actually venturing into public on Friday, March 18th, 2022, outfitted in what can only be described as a Ralph Lauren Purple Label outfit, flowing blue cashmere coat and brilliant white sweater, and dark woolen trousers, he did so to an audience carefully selected. An audience of some 200,000 reputedly civil servants, given the day off with strict instructions about how to spend it, served as the backdrop to this Ralph Lauren-for-a-Czar catwalk. Still, Putin kept a safe distance between himself and the adoring crowd.

Is the cloister the natural habitat of dictators? Putin's retreat into his prophylactic bunker, appearing only by himself, in a business suit and a tie, to address the Russian people, bears no resemblance to the bare-chested Slavic warrior of old. (At the time of writing there are rumors that Putin is hiding in a bunker. Somehow it seems appropriate that he follow in a not-so venerable tradition of bunker aficionados.)[24] Putin, bare-chested, angling, bare-chested, riding a horse. Bare-chested, as if he wanted to show himself in contradistinction to the flabbiness of the Big Mac-loving Trump—Putin's sculpted upper body the very incarnation of a vigorous heteronormative masculinity.

The Putin of old has been dispatched to the archive. The old image has been replaced with one of unaffected boardroom masculinity. In place of Putin the bare-chested warmonger, (Crimea, land grabs in Georgia), we have Putin the war manager. At the beginning of the war Putin feigned efficiency, reporting on the unstoppable progress the Russian forces were making. Putin fully expected Russian troops to be welcomed as liberators in Ukraine. When facts on the ground made that narrative more difficult to sustain and news (and the obvious reality) of Western sanctions undermined that narrative anyway, Putin assumed a defensive posture. Russia was under attack by the West. Putin sought to portray the effects of Western sanctions as an ideal opportunity for Russia, after a period of (necessary) hardship, to make itself economically independent. Putin did not explain how the Russian economy would suddenly flourish. He did, however, seek to boost his audience's faith in the cause that is "Mother Russia."

In place of the leader as *über*-man, vigorous in action, the Russian man as at home in the outdoors as a bear in the Siberian forest, was a figure who resembled a stern parent delivering bad news to his family—bad news of his own making. Suddenly, Putin morphed into an over-dressed parent presiding over a near-tragic family meeting. Either that, or you could mistake him for an expensively groomed salesman.

Zelensky, on the other hand, exudes no bare-chested machismo. He seems almost too wimpy for that. Instead, Zelensky's masculinity has more the feel of "The Office's" Steve Carell's Michael Scott. The "Servant of the People's" history teacher exhibits some of the same haplessness as Michael Scott's out of his depth pen pusher.

Watching Putin's TV addresses gives one a very different version of Michael Scott, perhaps an impossible one. Putin could only be Michael Scott if Michael Scott had money enough to wear a made-to-measure suit. If Michael Scott's nondescript office could be transformed into a germ-free, magnificently uncluttered boardroom—a remarkably unremarkable boardroom, a boardroom made memorable only by how unmemorable it is. A boardroom made for TV. All the audience must see is Putin. Everything else must fade into insignificance. Every appearance by Putin, each one of his meetings with his advisers, is broadcast for national and global consumption. Everything takes second place to Putin from the waist up. This is what a czarist photo op looks like. Unreal. Entirely lacking in authenticity.

In sharp contrast, Zelensky presents a bedraggled, overworked masculinity. Clad, as we said, mainly in his by now regulation military green T-shirt, on the street, mingling with his troops, looking at once thrilled to be in the heat of battle, or as close to it as he dares to get, Zelensky appears slightly lost. He has the appearance of one decidedly overwhelmed by the situation in which he finds himself. Because he does not quite understand how he got be where he is, Zelensky gives off the effect of a wildly disbelieving, but doggedly determined, history teacher suddenly promoted to principal of the most ill-disciplined high school in the district. Life, as John Lennon once remarked, is what happens while you're making other plans.

Zelensky is hardly the conventional template for a man among men. Certainly not in a time of war. The effectiveness of Zelensky's public presence may derive, then, not from his ability to enact a convincing masculinity. Instead, his effectiveness owes everything to his willingness to embrace his hapless-but-determined mid-managerial role. As if Zelensky were channeling his inner Harry Truman, on condition that we understand Zelensky as a leader whose charm owes everything to being overwhelmed. Watching Zelensky puts one in mid of a rather unnerving prospect: Michael Scott being airlifted from the offices of Dunder Mifflin in Scranton, PA, and commanded to use his mid-level managerial skills to conduct a war. "A war you're not allowed to lose, Michael," his entire nation whispers hoarsely in his ear.

Unsurprisingly, Zelensky seems visibly ill-suited for the role. Still, his enthusiasm will not be dimmed, nor will his must-do spirit be quelled. Real life is indeed much, much, stranger than fiction.

It is to his advantage that, unlike his Russian counterpart, Zelensky seems a poor fit with the role of national leader. We can all agree that he does not appear to have the physique for it. Mid-level managers have neither the incentive nor, quite frankly, the leisure time, to hit the gym. Certainly not hit it Putin-hard. An air of bemusement hangs over Zelensky, an air that cannot be shaken no matter that he has quickly learned the rhetoric of war that allows him to strike exactly the right note with his western neighbors and his far-off allies, from Paris to London to Seoul to Washington, D.C. Zelensky is not Dan Quayle, but that does not mean that he has entirely rid himself of the deer-in-the-headlights feel that hangs about him. It does help, however, that Zelensky is way smarter than Quayle, him of Mr. Gentlemanly Cs at Indiana University fame. In any case, Putin's no Lloyd Bentsen, and I mean that with all due deference to the late-Texas senator. Still, a palpable unease continues to hang around Zelensky. It is as though he is wondering, trying to understand exactly how could he have been thrust into this role? He intended only to play at being a real president when the fictional one offered no more avenues for his comic self to explore.

And now this. It matters not, Zelensky seems to have decided, needs must. In any case, Putin's war has thrown up a definite contrast. The warmonger, it turns out, was capable only of playing a macho man. He isn't really as dripping in machismo as he wanted the world to believe. He is just a former cab driver turned high-level bureaucrat who, now that the going's getting tough, has decided that management from behind a desk is more his style. Really. And so, like any overmatched bureaucrat, Putin has retreated to the safety of his desk.

The president who played the history teacher Goloborodko, on TV, by contrast, has quickly warmed to his TV role. Zelensky is now, in ways he could never have imagined, the "Servant of the People." To serve, he is learning, is to run the risk of dying. This is what Zelensky offers his people. Out of the commitment to service, there emerges an unlikely hero. Faced with the realities of war, one man's faux machismo is shown to be vacuous. It is one thing to play at being a macho man, but quite another to actually hold onto that bravado when the going gets tough. Where's Billy Ocean when you need him? "When the going gets tough, the tough get going." When the going gets tough, toughness for show takes itself off to a sequestered bunker. When the going gets tough, the tough head for the nearest Ralph Lauren store. Meanwhile, the mild-mannered history teacher has shown himself to possess an unexpected courage, albeit a courage that only comes hesitatingly into view.

So, there he is, Zelensky, on the streets of Kyiv. It is as though he were one of the many vital servants, so necessary to the efficient running of the household, that make Lord Grantham's Downton Abbey function, function with no show of fuss or bother. Like any good Englishman in a time of crisis, Zelensky has decided that its always best to keep a stiff upper lip.

And if he can't quite mange that, then he is at least determined to fake it for the cameras. Which is to say, for the moment that matters. For the Ukrainian people, for the world. Zelensky is no "Mr. Carson." He lacks "Carson's" grumpy gravitas. But, like "Carson," Zelensky seems the very picture of trustworthiness. So even though he fails the "Mr. Carson" test, Volodymir Zelensky will do nicely, thanks. And our Volodymir, with his insistently upbeat demeanor (how does he manage it?), has learned to turn a phrase or two very nicely, wouldn't you say?

Zelensky's determination to meet the demands of the moment began not only in his refusal to be escorted to safety, but in his request for military support. "Ammunition:" the future of Ukrainian sovereignty depended on the capacity of the nation to fight, as it were, fire with fire. Russian aggression could—can—only be repelled with Ukrainian firepower. Give me guns. Give me guns or give me death, pleads our latter-day Ukrainian Patrick Henry. Give me guns and bullets and anti-aircraft missiles, or I will die. Give me air cover, or ... Zelensky has not stopped asking since he made that first public request. As the war enters its second month and the situation in Ukraine becomes more desperate for its people, Zelensky has become less politic in his phrasing. With Russian bombardment relentless and as Ukraine's military resources prove insufficient in staving off the attacks, Zelensky has gone so far as to suggest that NATO's "being run by Russia."[25] Under circumstances less tragic, confronting an enemy less brazen, Zelensky's reprimand of forces who proclaim to be Ukraine's allies would sound cheeky. As though a lesser power had momentarily forgotten its place in the global order of things.

Not so, in this case.

And that's because of the enduring resonance of that first simple declarative sentence. Simple, but effective.

Effective for one reason above all others.

AUTHENTICITY

In certain circles, and here one has in mind academic ones, the issue of "authenticity" is often a fraught one. Sometimes it is, justifiably, subjected to critique. Academics are wary of authenticity, particularly as it pertains to matters of culture, ethnicity, and identity. Rightly so, because these issues bear directly on the kind of claims that follow from it—the kind of claims, as we know by now, inherent to ethno-nationalism. In the case of, say, ethnicity, the geo-political question of origin comes into play, which can easily lead to a debate about the culture of this or that community and who did this first or who invented that practice. Culture as ownership, as ownership that reflects the essence of a people.

Any, say, imitation or borrowing of a practice by a different or rival community is considered an act of appropriation or, worse, an act of violence against those who insist on their original ownership. Things become even more entangled when there is a contestation around the territory of a group, and as regards the territory—"homeland," "fatherland," "motherland"—it is safe to say that who can lay claim, irrefutably in its mind, to what piece of land is invariably the source of conflict. This is the logic of *Blut und Boden*. Here we need only invoke Crimea, Donbas, or Donetsk as an illustrative example where the rationale for invading a neighboring state can be justified in the name of "protecting" an ethnic minority (Russians) from an antagonistic majority (Ukrainians). In the terms of this logic, annexation is necessary to prevent the "genocide" of an ethnic community, especially if said majority is operating under the aegis of "Nazis," no matter that the leader of this majority is in fact Jewish and the son of Holocaust survivors. Authenticity is what the invading power says it is. The false clarity of myth-making, as we've already established. No matter that this authenticity that is not authenticity falters on the altar of truth. It might beggar belief. We know, however, from long and painful experience, that might makes right.

As such, the authenticity that is not fails what we can call the commonsense test of authenticity. The test of commonsense authenticity which can take the form of a very succinct question: Do I believe you? Simple. That answer can only be, in the commonsense that is authenticity, either "Yes," "*Ni*" or "*Nyet.*" Ukraine answered "*Так*," a "Yes" which would have needed no translation in neighboring Poland, a nation with its own deep and historic fear of Russia.

This brings us to the core of authenticity. That which is authentic is that which is presumed to be true. An authentic statement is that statement that cannot be disputed. An authentic person is that person whose word cannot be drawn into question. An authentic person is a person whom we believe. We take an authentic person at her or his word because there is no discrepancy between what the person says and that which we understand to be true. Authenticity = Truth. The authentic personage is, it turns out, a person, a political leader, that people will follow—who will risk their own death because he speaks the truth, the dire truth, of their nation's plight—a nation which the authentic leader not only speaks on behalf of, but, more importantly, comes to embody by virtue of his authenticity.

Authenticity will not abide the performative, the performative being an issue to which will return. What is authentic in its commonsense understanding is that speaking that requires no embellishment. Authenticity, if it is to remain true to itself, must show a decided preference for the everyday vocabulary. The more words used that are words which form part of everyday verbal interactions, that is, the more recognizable and trafficked in those words, the greater will be their effect. These words will resonate because they require no embellishment. These words, "I don't need a ride," reveal everything—which means that they disguise nothing. Authentic language, in Zelensky's case, is that language in which word and meaning are in perfect harmony.

Zelensky means what he says. Authentic language, very simply, *is* the truth. In authentic language, truth is revealed as truth. And the truth, so taken, is that language impatient with every word that is not the stuff—the building block and foundation of—of everyday speech. Into the category of the inauthentic we can put all language that is excessive, all language that dresses itself in superfluous, florid niceties. That is the language of specialization and all language that bears the mark of expertise, all language embraced and deployed by the educated, technocratic class, that language is treated with downright suspicion. That is, if it not dismissed out of hand. Authentic language, whatever the reservations of the chattering classes, is the only language that can be trusted.

In the moment of Ukrainian reckoning, Ukrainians found in Volodymyr Zelensky a leader who had in his command the language of authenticity. However, as former Ukrainian Prime Minister Oleksiy Honcharuk (2019-2020) insisted in an interview aired on National Public Radio (NPR) on March 15th, 2022, there is little doubt that the Ukrainian people would have risen to the occasion regardless. There is, of course, no way of establishing either the veracity or the accuracy of Honcharuk's claim, much as one would like to believe it to be true. What any political activist will attest to, however, is that it is much easier to rally people to a cause when activists ascribe truth (meaning, shared values, a common mode of life, and so on) to that cause. It never hurts, of course, if that cause also happens to have a leader who embodies, symbolizes, incarnates that cause, and can crystallize its truth. (Nor does a little charisma hurt.) If that truth can be crystallized globally, so much the better. All modes of being a leader that lends itself to authenticity. If the leader speaks the language of the people, if such a political aphorism might be permitted. In Zelensky, it seems that the capacity for motivation (rousing his people), the gift of language, and the aptitude for representation coincide.

Fortified by the language of authenticity, convinced of Zelensky's truth, Ukrainians girded themselves for battle. Into the breach. And those who could not, fled to safety.

A similar truth issues from "I need ammunition." Heroic resistance, "I don't need a ride," is followed hard by urgent admission. Lack. "I need" what I do not have. We need what you have. Apparently, it would require only 1% of NATO's arsenal to repel Russia. Zelensky's is already not only a request, but a question—more than a question—a moral appeal. A moral appeal that abuts on what was first, an implicit indictment. Life and death. A question that became an explicit indictment. In the form of "NATO's being run by Russia." And, if "NATO's being run by Russia," would South Korea please step in? Or, step up?

If the authentic self does not receive what it needs, it will die. It will die of lack. A lack that need not exist. 1%. (That percentage so infamous in American political life: the "1%." Which right-thinking person wants to throw in their lot with the "1%?" That is one thing. By contrast, who would not want to give to the militarily needy just "1%?") Authentic speech may derive from the self, but it is always addressed to the other. Authentic speech has no authenticity unless it is acknowledged by the other. The morality of authenticity is founded upon exchange between self and other. The self must be believed by the other otherwise the self's authenticity has no standing outside of itself. The other's belief in the self validates the self's authenticity. The other must give a sign, in word or deed, through an audible reply or through immanent action (which is also imminent action, in Zelensky's case), that it has heard what the authentic self says. The authenticity of the self must be validated by the other. The other testifies to the authenticity of the self. The other signs, signs off on, the self's authenticity.

THE COMMONSENSE OF AUTHENTICITY

Authenticity is when everything can, as it were, be taken at face value. When everything makes sense. Even, or, especially, when it affirms commonsense. But that does not mean that everything opposed to the authentic is that which flies in the face of commonsense.

Can we recall another leader, confronted with the threat of a hostile power bearing down on him, clearly targeting him, who would so confound our expectations? Any other leader would, at the first sign of trouble, have hopped onto the first available helicopter, military airplane, private jet. This one, instead, chose to stay. Not only to stay, but, at least symbolically, to stay and fight with his overmatched troops. This leader ditched his suit (while Putin surveyed his wardrobe), donned a military green T-shirt, and rallied not only the troops, but the entire nation.

This is surely the authenticity of the true revolutionary. One could easily imagine Ché Guevara behaving in a similar fashion, and happily, too—hair flapping beneath his trademark beret, beard coiffed to imperfection, urging his charges to launch themselves, once more, into battle. Or, Fidel, chomping on a cigar, cursing the *Yanquis*. Or, Patrice Lumumba, who would have encouraged his fellow-revolutionaries so in the most studied way. Or, maybe, Burkina Faso's Thomas Sankara, an assassinated leader who went to meet the guns hired to kill him, face to face.

However, Sankara, as we know, was not quite as authentic as we would wish him to be. Revolutionary that he was, vigorously anti-imperialist that he was, champion of the poor that he was, Sankara "muzzled the free press, imprisoned some opponents without trial and faced accusations of human rights abuses. In 1986 Amnesty International reported that a soldier had died in custody after being tortured with a blow torch."[26] Sometimes revolutionary authenticity isn't all it's cracked up to be. Sometimes the authentic and the inauthentic are bound up in the same person, unevenly distributed. Imperfection all round. After all, the revelations contained Pandora

Papers about Zelensky gave us reason enough to approach the authentic revolutionary with caution.

We have every reason to be cautious about an actor who rose to fame playing, of all things, a history teacher. History teaches us this. Master of authenticity he may be, Zelensky, but that does not mean he will act felicitously in all matters. We are right to worry that he might, after all Russia's violence against and destruction of his country, still "negotiate" a peace that is not a peace with Putin. A peace that could include a Ukraine divided, as Huang Rui feared, into an eastern and western Ukraine, with eastern Ukraine being absorbed into Russia.[27] (That would be disastrous, and not only for Ukraine. Zelensky recognizes this and recently declared himself opposed to any outcome that sought to divide Ukraine.[28]) Our caution, our wariness, however, will have to enter an uncomfortable relation with the commonsense of authenticity.

In any case, that is not how the common sense of authenticity works. First, this specific mode of common sense does not demand felicity. It is in some ways a febrile animal—nervous, excitable, maybe even a little unpredictable. Second, and this matters especially, the Pandora Papers speak of a leader himself capable of extracting wealth from the system he oversees; the logic of common sense understands that the revolutionary is a flawed human being, not a saint. As such, past—and even present—indiscretions, missteps (of which underestimating Putin's determination to invade ranks first), political shortcomings, these can all be accepted, dealt with, and, yes, they are frequently overlooked. But they must not be forgotten. Too much is riding on the outcome. Sceptics might advise us to sleep with half an eye open.

Regardless, the common sense of authenticity is, more than anything, attentive to the demands of the moment. Harping on past transgressions does nothing to address what is going on now, what is needed in this very instant.

THE METHOD IS NOT THE MAN

Nevertheless. Even as we forget, we must remember to remember. The Zelensky Method is not foolproof. The Method is not the man. The electoral accident of Golobordoko should serve as its own reminder. In history, accidents happen—and only some of those accidents have a fortuitous outcome. In fact, very few accidents in history secure a good result. Remembering this, no revolution should invest too much in a single individual. No revolution should sign itself over to such an individual, just because of the seductions of the commonsense of authenticity, seduced as we already are. Churchill, to whom we will turn in relation to Zelensky, was a great, inspiring war-time leader.

However, to secure the post-War Welfare State, Churchill, arch-Tory, unapologetic imperialist that he was, had to be consigned to history. A time, a place, for everything; for everything a season, its own logic of commonsense, and a logic worth keeping in mind. British Labour Prime Minister Harold MacMillan's "Winds of Change" speech, delivered in Cape Town, South Africa, to an all-white parliament, was a historical confrontation that Churchill could never have countenanced, let alone have given voice to. However reluctantly, MacMillan faced the truth that was the end of Empire. MacMillan gave that historic speech on February 3rd, 1960. Thirty years later, almost to the day, 2nd of February 1990, Nelson Mandela walked out of prison a free man. Mandela gave his first speech on Cape Town's Grand Parade, no more than a few hundred meters from where MacMillan had spoken. MacMillan spoke when the world, and apartheid South Africa in particular, was very different.

By contrast, in its capacity make sense of contradictions, the commonsense of authenticity is, if nothing else, pragmatic. It knows what it knows but it is in no way bound by what it knows.[29] Like everyone else, the authentic revolutionary is the product of our post-lapsarian world. The authentic revolutionary neither dwells upon nor denies his inauthenticity. But, because he is an authentic revolutionary and, as such, has no desire for martyrdom, the common sense of authenticity simply asks that the revolutionary live with the history of his transgressions. All the while committing to remembering those missteps. Storing them for a future date. A date that will surely arrive, a self-accounting that is inevitable.

THE UPSIDE OF MARTYRDOM

Martyrdom, of course, has its upside for the revolutionary. In death, Ché Guevara has become even more iconic than he was while he was alive fighting in the jungles of Africa and dying in the jungles of his native Latin America. Today Frantz Fanon is more widely read, in elite universities, among activists from Asia, Africa, the Caribbean, Europe, and the U.S., than he ever was in the brief 36 years of his life. All over the capital city of Ougadougou, there are works of art celebrating Sankara, to say nothing of the rest of Burkina Faso. A bronze statue of Sankara now stands in Ougadougou, right in front of the very place where he was assassinated. Cast in bronze, with his trademark ivory-engraved pistol (a gift from North Korea's Kim Il-sung) holstered at his right side, his left fist clenched defiantly, the Ougadougou statue memorializes a revolutionary, ensuring a historic afterlife. In death, if not in life, Sankara has triumphed over his former friend and bitter rival, Blaise Compaoré—the Burkinabe Brutus, Compaoré, the one-time friend turned plotter and executioner—while Compaoré lives in gilded isolation in neighboring Ivory Coast, exiled from his homeland, detested by large numbers of his fellow Burkinabe, Sankara stands unrivalled. The authentic allows always for the possibility of strategic forgetfulness.

The authentic can absorb, repress, and perhaps even forgive transgressions, large and small. The authentic is entirely capable of trafficking in historical amnesia. The authentic can abide contradictions. It asks only that the figure of authenticity be authentic, "real," relatable, a figure with whom everyone else—or almost everyone else—can easily identify.[30] It is not expected that the authentic figure be pure, unblemished, above reproach. No, not at all. In fact, if the authentic figure approximated such political innocence, it would make it impossible for everyone else to relate to such a figure. The authentic marks, then, the triumph of "keeping it real," as hip-hop vernacular would have it. Authenticity is, in this regard, almost anti-Biblical. It wants no part of the logic that prescribes "He who hath no sin, cast the first stone." Faced with the threat of invasion, living daily with the prospect of the annihilation of a people, when maternity wards are bombed, when food and water, to say nothing of secure shelter, are in short supply, all stones must be, in the spirit of the young David about to face Goliath, cast against the behemoth.

The Biblical David, we remember, was armed with nothing but a slingshot and a handful of pebbles. Stones have their uses. Moral indignation in the heat of battle is not one of those uses, not when a "centaur"—part man, part horse, conflated into one by a giant bear-like ego – is bearing down on you. So considered, Goliath may be too nice a name for "Bloody Vladdy" Putin. Goliath only wanted to win. He did not want to exterminate an entire people. Although Goliath was an epic figure, he did not seek to wipe a nation of 40 million people off the face of the earth. (Of course, David too is epic. A great deal depended upon his victory.) Much as it has been invoked to describe the conflict between Putin and the Ukrainian people, the David and Goliath analogy is hardly an accurate one, tempting as it may be to invoke it to register the imbalance of forces. Much as the figure of David is saturated in authentic resistance; and Biblically-sanctified too.

The authentic revolutionary is not required to overcome his transgressions, he is not expected to rise above his indiscretions, and he is certainly not asked to apologize for his misdemeanors. The force of the authentic is that it can absorb the inauthentic into itself. In fact, to be authentic is to have carnal knowledge, as it were, of the inauthentic. Anything else would be, not to put too fine a point upon it, pure inauthenticity. Surely nothing is more authentic and commonsensical than that?

This approach is, of course, the very essence of common sense. Simply because it knows something, something unsavory, in this case, does not mean that such knowledge has to be reactivated. Authenticity certainly does not understand itself to be bound by, bound to act in the terms of, that knowledge in the present. It is, after all, commonsense to know that that which is known—the past transgression—is of no possible use in the present. It makes sense to treat the present as an autonomous moment in which only that which can be of assistance is allowed voice. That which in any way limits the ability to act efficaciously in the present is forsworn, ignored, denied, even.

Nothing can be allowed to impinge upon the sovereignty of the present. Nothing can be allowed to take precedence over that which is desperately needed.

THE AUTHENTIC REVOLUTIONARY

Authenticity is a demanding, but not a picky, historical master. For all its capacity to live with contradictions, for all is proximity to the inauthentic, there remains the need for the authentic revolutionary to be a figure of probity. Not to get everything right, and certainly not all the time. Not to have lived a blemish-free life, far from it. It is expected, however, that the authentic revolutionary embody a set of moral principles and evince a set of fundamental human qualities. Among these qualities, decency, honesty, and humility are of the utmost importance.

Thomas Sankara, we remember, who dispensed with the colonial name imposed upon his country, "Upper Volta," and renamed it Burkina Faso, the "land of upright men," was alert to the demands of common sense. That is why he hitched rides on the planes of neighboring leaders to international conferences, that is why he sold the government's fleet of Mercedes limousines. Why indulge in German luxury vehicles when a run of the mill French Renault would do as well? This is the stuff of economic common sense. Puritanical in bent. Waste not, want not.

Out of the bedrock of commonsense, however, rose a vision of a future society, a vision given to us by the 33-year-old Sankara that is progressive by any contemporary measure: "Sankara introduced reforms that were years ahead of their time—a quota for women in government jobs, bans on forced marriage and genital cutting, and a campaign to plant 10 million trees and stave off desertification."[31]

Visionary, yes, but also utterly commonsensical, especially as it directly addresses the concerns of Burkinabe women and demonstrates an ecological consciousness long before it was either fashionable or so urgent a planetary matter. No reimagining a national future distinct from the present without recognizing how the needs of tomorrow must be a matter for today. Never put off until tomorrow what needs to be done today. Amilcar Cabral, who led the movement against Portuguese colonialism in Guinea Bissau and Cape

Verde, was similarly progressive in his championing of the rights of women not only in a future independent nation but in the revolution itself. Agro-ecologist that he was, Cabral was forever mindful of the agricultural needs of his people. That is why Cabral, trained as an agronomist in Portugal, took crop rotation in the zones liberated by his party, the PAIGC,[32] as seriously as he did military resistance to colonial occupation. As for Sankara, how many other national leaders took up the issue of "desertification" in the mid-1980s? How many societies, in Africa and beyond, committed themselves to ensuring greater representation for women in "government jobs" in that self-same period? It is a much more recent phenomenon.[33] How many other legislatures prohibited violence against the female body and forbade "forced marriages?"

Doesn't it all just seem like common sense?

THE WORK IT TAKES TO MAKE COMMON SENSE

Of course not, because what we take to be "common sense" is as much the consequence of difficult intellectual labor, the work it takes to produce a common understanding of how to be in the world, as it represents the harnessing of what we take, sometimes mistakenly, sometimes correctly, to be the only logical response to a set of circumstances. When we so blithely remark, "But that's just common sense," we do ourselves no justice. We have worked, that is, we have thought, often long and hard, about what we understand to be shared by us as a species. Whatever is common to us all, is what we have made so.

Fighting "deforestation," Sankara recognized, was going to be a major environmental and political issue for his landlocked nation with very little water. Providing food for a revolutionary army and securing a food supply for an independent African people was for Cabral a simple fact of life. Fighting environmental degradation, as everyone in Brazil's rainforest would readily attest, tending carefully to water reserves, as coastal cities as far apart as Cape Town, South Africa, and Chennai, India, would be quick to remind us (as both cities faced the very real prospect of drought just a few short years ago), has now become the world's business.

Common sense is that mode of being, that received wisdom, that everyday thinking that we routinely engage in but do not consciously acknowledge, that we practice without recognizing how it is we have come to share this body of acknowledge. A thinking out of order in order to produce an ordered, commonsensical thinking. How what we take to be involuntary reflexes, quotidian modes of exchange, our shared understanding of what it takes to address a particular situation, is in fact an outcome secured by a long process of intellectual contemplation. What we so glibly understand as "common sense" is the product of how it is we have trained ourselves to think about how it is we are, how it is we would like to be, in the world.

Common sense is thus both, in the same instant, an unconsidered reflex and an intellectual achievement.

When we speak so easily of "common sense," we both sell ourselves short—"It is only common sense"—and fail to recognize how much it is that we still need to make "common" amongst us. Such as the probity required to lead a nation. The very probity that will not permit of attacking defenseless civilians, the probity that will check our impulse to threaten nuclear disaster. It should, after all, be commonsense that one cannot deactivate a nuclear reactor once it's been activated.

Part of NATO and the U.S.'s reluctance to impose a "no-fly zone" over Ukraine is that it could trigger a nuclear war. A terrifying prospect that must be considered, that must always be part of every decision taken in relation to this war. In terms of the realities of geo-politics, an explicable decision, but not enforcing a no-fly zone is at the expense of Ukrainians lives; and, as millions of Ukrainians are made refugees by Russia's war, now have to live with the reality of a destroyed way of life because the Russian military, whatever its other deficiencies, still enjoys air superiority. It is for this reason that Zelensky, in an interview in mid-April, accused his would-be allies of lacking the "guts" to help Ukraine against Russia.[34] It takes a lot of courage, it would appear, to do the right thing. When the world promises "never again," Zelensky insists, in relation to Auschwitz and Buchenwald, it really does not really mean "never again."

How is it that the danger of nuclear disaster is not common knowledge at the highest echelon of the Kremlin? How is it that tens of thousands of Serbs can protest in favor of Russia in Belgrade?[35] How is it that Montenegro is a safe harbor for the Russian oligarchs' yachts? (Anything offensive Serbia[36] can do, we can do better? Or, worse, as the case might be? Is that the logic, Montenegro?) How is that the United Arab Emirates abstains from condemning Russia at the UN? How is it that Saudi Arabia continues to provide a haven for the ill-gotten gains of Russian oligarchs? As Italy seizes the yachts of Putin's cronies,[37] Saudi Arabia provides a safe port for them to dock? How is it that Bermuda prohibits Russian-owned aircraft from landing at its airports while Montenegro[38] is suddenly chock-a-block with very large, and very expensive yachts? Superyachts, even? How is it that China stands belligerently on the side of Putin? Why is Israel allowing private jets, newly arrived from St. Petersburg, carrying oligarchs, no doubt, to park at Ben Gurion airport?[39] The ironies compound.

While the Ukrainian Jew Zelensky is trying to save his people from Russian bombardment, Israel plays host to Russian oligarchs, not least among them Jews who have long cozied up to Putin, Jewish oligarchs such as Roman Abramovich, a Putin crony about whom we will have more to say shortly. Suffice it to say for now that Abramovich's plaything is not a yacht, but a "superyacht," and it is named "Solaris." It's worth a cool $600 million and its now docked in Montenegro.[40]

In addition to Abramovich's "Solaris"[41] and Putin's "Graceful," there are also the grandiloquently named "Galactica Super Nova," owned by Vagit Alekperov (a yacht name that almost invites a joke about cosmic explosions; it would even be funny, a joke about exploding stars, that is, if Mariupol, even more than Kyiv, did not resemble a postapocalyptic moonscape after more than a month of continuous bombardment), and a name which is at once ironic and deeply offensive, the "Amore Vero," owned by Igor Sechin. Only a truly cynical oligarch would name his superyacht "love of truth." There are other superyachts, but "Clio" and "Luna" just don't have the same catchy ring to them. "Amore Vero" is the hands down winner in the best in cynicism class. (Attached is map so you can see where they're docked. Everywhere in the world from the Maldives to Antigua.)[42]

Jewish oligarchs who have benefited from the Kremlin's largesse are now seeking safer harbors—literally, in some cases, as they try to prevent their multi-million-dollar yachts from being impounded—where they can ensure the safety of their assets. What a united front they present, a rare moment of Middle Eastern/Gulf agreement. An Israel-UAE alliance, one to confound the critics, to befuddle a logic previously founded upon historic enmity and religious difference.

S-U-I

A new political moniker has entered our vocabulary: I-S-U, Israel, Saudi Arabia, the United Arab Emirates. The hyphen insisted upon because all three partners want the benefit of plausible deniability. However, there may already be an extant abbreviation of which they can avail themselves, and a fitting one it might be too: SUI, the international abbreviation for Switzerland. Apropos? Yes, and no. Yes, because *SUI* gives ideological cover. Even in the case of the worst humanitarian crises, Switzerland has insisted on its right to neutrality. Not anymore. Even for the Swiss Russia's invasion is a bridge too far, the atrocities in Bucha (a suburb just outside of Kyiv in which Ukrainian corpses have been found, some of them with their hands bound and executed, mobster—or, Nazi—style) making the money too unclean for even the usually conscience-free Swiss to touch.

While the Swiss say *assez*, or *genug*, or *abbastanza*, among their many ways of saying "Enough," from Israel there came appeals, from the nation's highest institutions, to give Abramovich a pass. *The New York Times* reports,

> As Russian troops massed near the border with Ukraine last month, the American ambassador to Israel received an appeal on behalf of Roman Abramovich, the most visible of the billionaires linked to President Vladimir Putin.
>
> Leaders of cultural, educational, and medical institutions, along with a chief rabbi, had sent a letter urging the United States not to impose sanctions on the Russian, a major donor, saying it would hurt Israel and the Jewish world.[43]

Such a request is explained easily enough. Self-interest, no matter that it is dressed as a larger concern. Israel's Prime Minister Naftali Bennett has thus far refused to condemn Russia, which has led to criticism of Israel by, among others, Zelensky and members of the US Congress.[44] The U.S., for so long Israel's staunchest international ally, is finding out just how narrow Israeli self-interest trumps everything, including Israel's refusal to condemn Russia at the UN. No matter how it represents its neutrality, Israel, like South Africa, Brazil, and India, to say nothing of the usual dictatorial suspects, a list that includes the likes of Syria, North Korea, and Eritrea, must be designated complicit in Russia's war on Ukraine. Israel, to whom Zelensky directly appealed, as a fellow-Jew, in addressing the Knesset, met with occasional approval, but mainly his appeal fell on deaf ears. Instead, when Zelensky raised the prospect of another Shoah, he found himself taken to task for his impertinence (How dare he?), to phrase the matter politely.

Conveniently dismissed in the Knesset's refusal to condemn Putin, was the effects of Russia's war for the Ukrainian people. Zelensky, it seemed, could hardly believe what was unfolding before him when he found himself under attack after his address to the Knesset. And rightly so. For all the members of the Knesset's bellicosity, posturing and righteous indignation, feigned, of course, as righteous indignation as a rule tends to be, the common-sense truth remained unarguable. After all that gnashing of Knesset teeth, what of the violent crackdowns against Russian opposition (Alexei Navalny, for one, imprisoned, poisoned, his supporters denied the right to protest, exiled)? What of the repression of free speech which include attacks on journalists, the looting of state coffers, the attacks on neighboring states (first Georgia, now Ukraine)? Does that count for nothing?

Will there be an apology forthcoming, at some distant point in the future, from Israel, South Africa, India, to the tens of thousands of Ukrainian dead? Has not the world learned, as the Jewish world knows all too well, that *post ipso facto* apologies contain at their core a certain hollowness? Just ask the victims of the deadliest war in human history, still raging today in the Great Lakes region of Africa. Countless other peoples would be only too willing to attest to this truth. The victims know that an unpunctual *mea culpa* is often nothing more than the denial of a truth that was known in the moment of the tragedy. Is not the "hurt" of the moment that confronts us all the one to which we must attend, with all undue haste, with all the urgency we can muster?

This "hurt" overlooks Ukrainian victims, the dead and the maimed. To say nothing of those mutilated bodies in Bucha (which not only rhymes with "butcher," as in Putin the "Butcher of Bucha,"[45] but brings to mind that other great atrocity, "Buchenwald"), those bodies lying in the rubble of the nation's cities that cannot be buried because of Russia's relentless attack. A "hurt" which refuses to see the greatest number of refugees in Europe since World War II, Ukrainians made refugees because every Ukrainian city has been laid siege to; that is, if it not has not been laid to waste. What say these Israeli cultural institutions and that chief rabbi who seeks to immunize Abramovich about this? About bombed Kyiv? About the threat of nuclear war? Tens of thousands of Ukrainians made to join, against their will, an exodus? What of the fate of those diasporized into neighboring European nations? Or dissident Russians seeking shelter in not only nearby Armenia but in Israel itself?

Refugees and dissidents, victims of an entirely different order, find themselves in the same desperate situation, all made to depend upon the kindness of neighbors. What of that? What is it to those in power in Tel Aviv, Riyadh, Pretoria, Dubai? How can Tel Aviv yoke itself to Moscow? How do those who consider themselves observant Jews, Christians, or Muslims countenance such horror, a horror that derives from a mode of being in the world that is more Darwinian than in any way faithful to any monotheistic tenets? A line of thinking that hews to the logic that only those who tend to their own self-interest will survive.

What faith can sustain itself if it considers the "hurt" that it might incur before it tends to the death that is being visited, in great numbers, upon the other?

What faith is devoid of the principle of self-sacrifice?

"For God so loved the world that He gave his only begotten Son." This is a Christian truth, radical in its commitment to self-sacrifice. This is the very instantiation of grace. Grace, we should know, is beyond us human beings. Grace is what God showed us by sacrificing his "only begotten Son." In a word, grace is love beyond love. Grace is that love of which only God is capable. He allowed his Son to die on the cross. Dying on a cross, flanked on either side by common thieves. God, one knows if one is of the Christian persuasion, God knew the deepest hurt.

That act of grace is what Pope Francis, direct descendant of St. Peter, seems to have put aside.

"The Man Who Flew Into Space From His Apartment" by D. James Dee. NY, Ronald Feldman Gallery 1998. Copyright: Ilya & Emilia Kabakov. Courtesy of Ilya & Emilia Kabakov.

ROMAN CATHOLIC FAILURE, ON THE ORDER OF THE JESUITICAL

In refusing to defend the lives of the Ukrainian people, all the countries who reveal themselves as fellow-(Russian)-travelers have Ukrainian blood on their hands. They are co-constructors in the impossible project that is *Russky Mir*, the making-Russian of the world. At the very least, they do nothing to oppose that project. These fellow-travelers are joined, ignobly, in this regard, by Pope Francis. The current Pontiff issues—like his World War II predecessor, Pius XII, whose broad condemnations provided cover to Hitler and Mussolini—categorical denunciations of the war, calls for "peace,"[46] in his Easter Sunday 2022 address to the faithful gathered in St. Peter's Square criticizes Russia's invasion as a "cruel and senseless war," but refuses to name the culprit-in-chief, Putin. In a pathetic effort to defend himself, Francis instead accuses journalists who point out his Pius XII-like silence of "coprophilia"[47] – a sexual fetish for feces.

There is good reason to believe that Francis' reluctance to condemn Putin has everything to do with his determination to repair the centuries-old breach between Eastern and Western Christianity, a breach that goes back to 1054. Francis took the first steps in that mission when he and Patriarch Kirill, head of the Russian Orthodox Church, met in Cuba in 2014. To condemn Putin, in Francis' calculations, would be to castigate Kirill. Better to accuse unsympathetic journalists of talking crap than to speak aloud the name of a faux-faithful Orthodox Russian leader.

Only one common sense Christian question presents itself: Why not? Why give comfort, not tacit but explicit, to Kirill? After all, the Patriarch repeatedly makes clear not only his support for Putin, but has sanctified Russia's war in Ukraine. A Holy War in the cause of *Russky Mir*—the recolonization, the taking back, in Kirill and Putin's political calculus, of what the god of Orthodoxy has ordained Russia's. The Grand Empire of Mystical Orthodoxy. What kind of Roman Catholicism countenances the death of tens of thousands in the name of conciliation with a church that advocates death to

Ukrainians? Why would Francis side with an Orthodox church that lauds Putin because it sees him, as Kirill does, as the last line of Christian defense against the great liberal scourge that is the LGBTQ+ movement?

Kirill has named Putin a "miracle of God," the political leader of Russian Orthodoxy who will stay, forever, one presumes, the horrific spectacle of "gay parades" on the streets of St. Petersburg and Moscow. Kirill's Orthodox "miracle worker" is the architect of Ukrainian death. All this careful politicking by Francis, minding his Ps (for Putin, no doubt) and Qs in relation to Putin and Kirill, during the holiest month of the Christian calendar. Compared to Francis, St. Peter was merely an indecisive ditherer when he thrice denied Jesus-the-Christ to the Roman soldiers. Putin is but the latest in a long line of political figures who recognize the inherent advantages of the mystical tradition in Orthodox Christianity.

While the Jesuit from Buenos Aires, Francis, insists only general declamation ("peace," "an end to the war," "cruel and senseless"), in Poland and Ukraine bishops have taken it upon themselves to speak the commonsense truth of the Russian invasion. For his part, "Bishop Stanislav Szyrokoradiuk of Odessa-Simperopol in Ukraine ... wanted stronger words from Francis about Kirill, who, the bishop said, 'blesses this new Hitler and Russian fascism.'"[48] Where is Francis' command of this manner of straight talk? The Odessa-Simperopol bishop's courage and clarity finds a poetic resonance in Polish Archbishop Stanislaw Gadecki's faith in the final judgment that awaits Putin. A judgment that will surely not look at all kindly on Francis and Kirill. "'[E]ven if someone manages to avoid this human justice,'" Gadecki reminds the Christian faithful, "'there is a tribunal that cannot be avoided'" (Ibid). There is something historically fitting that it is Gadecki, a Pole, reminding Francis of his bounden duty.

After all, Francis was supposed to be the Pontiff whose papacy marked a return to a radical, more egalitarian Roman Catholicism, one infused by the left-leaning liberation theology that spread across Latin America in the 1970s and 1980s. Archbishop Jorge Mario Bergoglio's election to the papacy was an historic event. Not only the first Jesuit (Society of Jesus is their proper name), but also the first pope from the Americas and the first from the southern hemisphere. (It was if Francis' rise to the papacy in 2013 fulfilled, but not quite, Fidel Castro's prediction about the moment in which the U.S. would engage in dialogue with communist Cuba. "The U.S. will talk to us when they have a black President and the world has a Latin American pope." There might have been thaw in U.S.–Cuba, relations, but hardly a breakthrough moment of *détente*. When Francis became pope Barack Obama was in his second term in office. Two out of three isn't bad.) Roman Catholics hoped to find in Francis signs of a Church returning to a man of thought. A reasonable expectation, given that Jesuits founded the most prestigious universities in Roman Catholicism. But Roman Catholics also hoped that they had found a pastor faithful to Jesuitical principles such as the alleviation of poverty. A sense of expectation that rose when Borgoglio took "Francis" for his papal name, in honor of St. Francis of Assisi. Born at the latter end of the 12th century, Francis of Assisi underwent a religious conversion which caused him to forswear his rich, carefree life in favor of a life of poverty. Catholics of a liberal and radical persuasion hoped that they found in this first Jesuit pope a pastor who prized equality and justice and who was a freer thinker than his doctrinaire predecessor, Benedict XVI.

After all, the Jesuits, an order founded in 1540 by the Spanish soldier, Ignatius Loyola, pride themselves on a history of opposing Rome's authority. An intellectual order, the largest in the Roman Catholic church, Jesuits are bound by a contradiction: they are not supposed to seek higher office, but, at the same time, they must be loyal to the church and obey its authority. Jesuits have, until Francis' election, been faithful to the former, and, to their eternal credit, not so observant of the latter.

No wonder then that the faithful were heartened, upon Francis' election, to learn that the Archbishop of Buenos Aires boasted a common touch. He supported his local football club in Buenos Aires, San Lorenzo, rather than either of the city's big two clubs, Boca Juniors or River Plate. Francis rode the bus to his office. Using public transportation to get to work presented a sharp contrast with his predecessor, the German, Benedict XVI.

Cardinal Joseph Ratzinger is less affectionately known as "God's Rottweiler" because of his determined opposition to Vatican II (convened by John XXII in 1962 and closed, four sessions later, by Paul VI in 1965). In this meeting of the Second Ecumenical Council, the Roman Catholic church sought to make the Church relevant for its twentieth-century flock. The most enduring change which Vatican II effected was allowing the mass to be conducted in vernacular languages, i.e., not Latin, as had been the case up to that moment. Like his immediate predecessor, the Pole John Paul II, Ratzinger was a conservative who worked to undo the radical inclination of Vatican II. Or, to put the matter plainly: Benedict XVI sought to complete the project of undoing the radical propensities of Vatican II that the dogmatic John Paul II, who belonged to the Dominican order, had begun.

John Paul II, who did everything he could to stamp out dissent in the Church, excising from authority all those within the Church hierarchy who disagreed with or questioned his doctrinal stance. Not surprisingly, John Paul II, considered by many to have been autocratic in his papal dispensation, was especially intolerant of the Jesuits. The Jesuits were a thorn in John Paul's side. The Polish Pope, who ascribed to the notion of papal infallibility, did everything in his power to quash Jesuit dissent. He would not brook Jesuit intellectual challenges, or, indeed, any intellectual challenge, as Catholic theologians such as Hans Jüng (a Swiss theologian with whom Ratzinger studied at the University of Tübingen in the years 1966-69) and Charles Curran soon learned. John Paul II was especially intolerant with the democratic impulse of Vatican II—he made his unhappiness with the rise of liberation theology in Latin America known, rebuked those Catholics who supported it, and worked assiduously to stymy any attempts to decentralize the Church.[49] Not surprisingly, Benedict XVI canonized his predecessor. The miracle that John Paul performed, one imagines, was the Polish Pope bringing down communism. Now officially known as "Saint John Paul," or, as his conservative loyalists would surely prefer, "John Paul the Great;" his miracle, in the Church's version of (validation for) his canonization was that he cured a French nun, Marie Simon Pierre, of Parkinson's.

However, to his credit, one can say that, unlike his successor, the Benedictine Ratzinger, John Paul had no taste for the finer things in life such as red ermine slippers. Exclusive, designer fashion—that was Ratzinger's thing. Small comfort.

Pope Benedict XVI's was, mercifully, a short reign. A signal one, too. He was the first pope to resign since Gregory XII in 1415, and the first to do so of his own volition since Celestine in 1294. (Mired in scandal, Pope Celestine jumped just as he about to be pushed.) By Celestine's standards, then, Benedict is an honorable Pope Emeritus. But only by Celestine's standards, because Benedict XVI (2005-13) was heavily criticized for his handling of the sexual abuse cases which came to light during his papacy and upon which he failed to act with any authority; or, one might propose, without any clear moral purpose. Apologies were offered to the victims, and financial restitution was made. That, however, was only in part what the sexual abuse scandals were about, wasn't it? It was about those who, understood by their congregants to be servants of the Church, acted against the most vulnerable members of their congregation. And, protected by the power of the Church, they felt empowered to act as they wished, with almost no fear of retribution. The Church, for the longest time, and probably still, protected those in their ranks.

BENEDICT XVI, BENEDICT OF NURSIA

Unlike Borgoglio, the German Ratzinger, an anti-Nazi native of Bavaria who deserted from Hitler's army, was very much a man of Europe. Ratzinger took the name Benedict not only to honor Benedict XV (1914-22), who sought to mediate between the combatants in the Great War, but to acknowledge Benedict of Nursia, the patron saint of Europe. (Situated in the Italian province of Perugia, Nursia is now more commonly known as "Norcia." The town is in the region of Umbria.) The scholar Ratzinger understood his work to be revitalizing the Church in Europe. Because the missionary calling is central to the Jesuits, Francis is, if not personally then through Jesuitical osmosis, more a man of the world; that is, the world beyond Europe's borders. With Francis' rise to the papacy, the College of Cardinals, which elects the pope, whatever its grave historical limitations, signaled a rupture in precisely the fabric that Benedict XVI had sought to keep whole. In 2013, the Church found itself headed by a priest who would have been unrecognizable to Benedict of Nursia, the son of Roman nobleman who founded the Benedictine order. (At the very least, Ratzinger's membership in the Benedictine order might explain his taste for the finer things in life. On the other hand, maybe not. Francis of Assisi too was of noble birth. And much indulged by his family until he received his vision.)

"FRANCIS"

In choosing the name "Francis" for his papal self, the Jesuit Borgoglio brought together his religious deep-thinking order with that of the Franciscans, an order in which renouncing worldly things instills in its members a commitment to simplicity and sharing, of all kinds— worldly possessions, love, experience. For Franciscans, those values are the fundamental tenets of their faith. Quite an amalgam, Francis' choice of papal name. Intellectuality, a commitment to critique that does not shy away from ruffling the feathers of authority, complicated by the understanding that service to self-same Church that it subjects to scrutiny; joined to an order in which the dedication to simplicity (poverty is a virtue) and a recognition that all human beings are reliant on God's mercy are paramount.

Francis, it would seem, has abrogated the foundational elements of both orders. Francis does the Franciscans no honor when he turns a blind eye to a simple, commonsense truth: he will not share in the suffering of the Ukrainian people. He will not give them so much as rhetorical comfort because he will not name, let alone indict, the perpetrator of violence against his fellow-human beings. The bond that Francis shares, or hopes to share, with Kirill, suggests that the gesture of taking the name of an order other than his own is, to be reductive, about being politic. That is, it extends toward the other order only in name, not in essence. That is, in the moment of record, it turns from the truth embedded in the name "Francis."

In his self-fashioning as first a populist Archbishop and then as a populist, ecumenical pope (washing the feet of Christian, Hindu, and Muslim prisoners in 2016),[50] Francis has always been able to rely on the common touch. When he washed the feet of the refugees, he did so in the name of peace and fraternity. On at least five occasions, Francis has held mass in prison, and there too he engaged in the feet-washing ritual.

As moving, and, it must be said, as reassuring as such an act of papal humility might be, it is difficult not to be at least a little cynical in view of what the self-styled populist pope has so glaringly failed to do—to name the perpetrator. The perpetrator who is acting without regard for human life. The Gospel of St. James puts great store by the work that Christians do. Paul's Gospel, while by no means averse to works, reminds us repeatedly—all those carefully scripted Letters, all the apostolic fervor that suffuses Paul's epistles—of the power of the Word. Of the need for the Word to be spoken. Paul staked his life, in his epic wanderings, on the power of the Word to affect the world. Paul, as is well-known, possessed a zealotry unmatched in the New Testament. A zealotry that puts one in mind of the rectitudinous of Cecil John Rhodes' colonialist impulse. "Give me your Jews," Paul thunders, "Give me your Gentiles, I will bring them all to Christ." Paul was exceedingly sure, sometimes terrifyingly so, of his proselytizing mission.

It is, however, as the apostle who never wavered in his faith in the Word that Paul should, in a moment when the fate of the Ukrainian people is on the line, offer himself as the model on which Francis should draw.

It may be, however, that Francis inclines more to the disciple Peter on the morning of Jesus-the-Christ's crucifixion. Except denial takes the form of silence. But its effect is no different. Death follows, whether it is Peter refusing his affiliation with Jesus-the-Christ or Francis using generalities to avoid naming Putin. To date I am only aware of two occasions on which Francis has called for peace without denouncing Putin. We should expect the third betrayal to follow shortly, if it has not already happened. Betrayal of the Word comes a little more easily to Francis than faith in the Pauline Word.

Moreover, not only does Francis fail the Franciscans—Borgoglio is certainly a poor Jesuit too, given his refusal to publicly call either Putin or Kirill to account. Ukraine would appear to be the hill on which Jesuit thinking, the fealty to relentless inquiry, the search for veracity, and the genetic predisposition to question authority, dies. If anything, Francis is a profound negative example: Jesuits are sworn to keep their distance from power. Francis is living proof of why. Power neuters the greatest asset of the Order of Jesus. Intellectual militancy, what I would name thinking, and a distrust of authority are displaced by accommodationism—thinking is replaced by rationalization.

We should not, however, be surprised by Francis' inaction in relation to Putin and Kirill. Indeed, it is perhaps only a so poor in Ignatius' spirit a Jesuit as Francis who can ascend to the papacy. That is, a Jesuit who has long since accommodated himself to the machinations of power, a Jesuit Roman Catholic priest possessed of a reactionary bent. After all, when he became pope, stories began circulating again about his failure to act against state authority during the *guerra sucia*, the "dirty war," in his native Argentina. Francis, the line of criticism goes, did not speak up for truth and the sanctity of human when he was Archbishop of Buenos Aires. He might even have been culpable in the death of his members of his order. The lives laid waste by the military junta, bodies dumped from helicopters into the River Plate, children orphaned by the junta who conveniently "found" adoptive parents for them—childless couples in its own ranks. Opposition to the dictatorship crushed, violently. When liberation theology swept through Latin America, Francis, like John Paul II but unlike many in his order, would not embrace it. A company man, then, a company man, now. Countenancing the death of those who resisted, then, refusing to condemn those who seek to destroy a people seeking desperately to hold onto their way of life, now. It matters not, finally, what the preferred mode of transportation for a Jesuit Archbishop is. Eschewing a chauffeured car to ride the bus to work strikes us now, in the moment, again, when human life is at stake, as performative.

Riding the bus for show. A show of feigned democracy: Archbishop Borgoglio, priest of the people. Not fake, just feigned; pretending to be of the common people but when push came to shove, the Archbishop sided with power. Borgoglio's common touch, then, meant very little in relation to the violence of the military junta which in 1976 overthrew the government of Evita Peron. Led by Jorge Videla, Emilio Massera and Orlando Agosti, the junta waged a brutal campaign against those they designated "leftists" or "communists." Faced with the reality of unjust authority, Borgoglio failed to speak out against an illegitimate, dictatorial power. And so, the pattern was set.

However, it mattered then, as it matters now, that Francis act in the terms of his order. A lesson twice not learned. When the Jesuit priest, Archbishop, or the first Jesuit pope, fails to uphold the founding tenets of his order, it is those who stand for a common sense justice and who fight for the right to live, who show up the insubstantiality of the Archbishop of the diocese riding on a Buenos Aires bus. It is difficult, then, not to be at least a little suspicious when Francis holds up a Ukrainian flag sent to him from Bucha as a symbol of Russian violence.[51]

The common touch, sharing the experience of everyday (humble) transportation is nothing but pure spectacle; of the low rent variety, granted, but spectacle still. What matters is what the Jesuit Francis does when power threatens those who will not abide the abuse of power. When those who demonstrate a Jesuitical intellectual force, question authority, find themselves made vulnerable by their intellectual and physical courage. What a pretty pass things have come when a Polish bishop, nurtured in the conservative Catholicism of John Paul II's Poland, is that member of the Church hierarchy who speaks truth, fearlessly; when a Ukrainian bishop bears faithful witness to what is commonsense to all in his country. Putin, and Kirill, each in their own way, are instruments of violence. Neither the Russian president nor the Orthodox Patriarch could, commonsensically, claim to be instruments of peace. It is thus not only the Dominican pope, John Paul II, who threatened the truth and integrity of the Order of Jesus. Turns out the Jesuit who has reached the highest office in Roman Catholicism in the Order's history has a past and a present that brought and now brings fresh shame upon his fellow-Jesuits.

LAUNDROMAT LONDON. REPUTATION LAUNDERING

Why would so many leaders in Israel, in so many different walks of life, expend so much political capital on one man? Why were these powerful people so willing to excuse Roman Abramovich's very public, and, in truth, quite brazen, transgressions?

After all, there is a term for what Abramovich did with his money. And it is by no means a flattering one. Roman Abramovich engaged in reputation laundering. The British capital has long been known as Laundromat London. The city has earned this moniker because the nation's leaders, especially but not exclusively the Conservative Party (Tory), have studiously turned a blind eye to Russian oligarchs buying up huge numbers of swanky properties, especially in the boroughs of Kensington and Chelsea. Laundromat London: where dirty money can be washed clean. Money flows into Tory coffers, a little for the Labour Party, and everyone's content. Until now. The cultural corollary to money laundering is reputation laundering. Russian oligarchs determined to wash their reputations of their Kremlin stains, become benefactors for the arts. (Here it might be better to just call the reputation launderers "Kremlingarchs.") They donate to museums, have wings named after them. (The opioid crisis, Big Pharma and the Sacklers, anyone? Patrons of the arts, philanthropic benefactors, the Sacklers offer an appropriate analogy because the family traces its roots to Ukraine and Poland.) They bequeath to hospitals. They make themselves over into figures of beneficent largesse. They seek to keep their squalid pasts well out of sight as they strive to join respectable society. Musicians play at their birthday parties and their children's weddings (Beyoncé, J-Lo, Enrique Iglesias, Sting, to name but a few), artists find new champions (and new sources of funding), designers find an entirely novel coterie of the rich to model their merchandise. For some, of course, all this is not enough. They need a football club as well. There is no depth to which the dark arts, of which Abramovich is a master practitioner, will not descend.[52]

So, SUI generis is no longer sui generis. It's *SUI nouveau*, a veritable rogues gallery of economic opportunists that gathers into its embrace Tel Aviv, Riyadh, and Dubai, all happily exchanging titbits about a bunch of newly arrived, well-heeled Russian speakers who are looking to purchase property in their respective cities' most expensive neighborhoods. Welcoming the *SUI nouveau*, congratulating themselves, in all these cities, on making the gift of hospitality. Not a gift, exactly, but a profitable transaction for all concerned. The gift that keeps on taking. But because the "Kremlingarchs" have so much, they hardly notice when a million or eight go missing.

On second thoughts, then, it might be better to stick with I-S-U. And not because, as we said, even historically neutral Switzerland can abide what Putin is doing. This is Switzerland's famous First Stand. What dictators and kleptocrats have for centuries been unable to do, Putin's accomplished. The Swiss flag has been planted. Nothing on the order of a William Tell-led rebellion, but once even a smidgeon of that 14th century spirit has been reactivated, would it be too much to hope for tyrannicide to spread east?

Meanwhile, capital has found a new place to park those riches that want to vanish without a trace. Legally stashed, but, protected by anonymity and the Russian dolls strategy that is shell companies. Protected by the law of neutrality. Those days are gone, say the newly backboned Swiss, like Heidi, a pigtailed picture of innocence, who once roamed idyllic, hilly pastures in rustic isolation. Nothing to worry about, however, because capital has already found its new (economic) safe space. Welcome to the world of *SUI nouveau*. It has a ring to it, even it does grate on the Ukrainian ear.

BRICS: BRAZIL, RUSSIA, INDIA, CHINA, SOUTH AFRICA

Such a *mise-en-scène* inspires disgust of Homeric proportions, disgust of the kind Athena denounced when she witnessed Penelope's suitors staking claim, unashamedly, to everything in the absent Odysseus' home. Food, drink, entertainment, and, of course, the ultimate prize, the widow-who-is-not-a-widow but is husbandless nonetheless, Penelope herself. Observing all of this, and trying to counsel Telemachus, Penelope and Odysseus' son, Athena remarks:

> "Why any man of sense
>
> who chanced among them would be outraged,
>
> seeing such behavior."[53]

How is it that Brazil, India, and South Africa stand with Putin's violence? Why are these nations' leader not "outraged,/seeing such behavior?" Instead, the South African government of anti-apartheid veteran Cyril Ramaphosa dissembles. As every thinking South African knows, Ramaphosa's behavior is part of a pattern. After all, Ramaphosa knows a thing or two about oligarchical ambitions. He is adept enough at protecting his own self-interest. The death of the Marikana miners is proof enough of that.[54] Those deaths familiarized Ramaphosa with the feel of blood on his hands. In the vain attempt to cover up his blood-stained hands, Ramaphosa lashes out at the UN, decreeing the UN an "outdated body."[55] In Ramaphosa's logic, the UN is good for condemning apartheid. Nettlesome, meddlesome (surely?) and antiquated, however, when it comes to Russia's war against Ukraine.

Post-apartheid South Africa will not condemn Russia, the long-ago trade unionist Ramaphosa insists, because Russia sided with South Africa's disenfranchised black majority during apartheid. Just plain geo-politically wrong, say saner, more ethical voices in South Africa. It was the Soviet Union that was steadfast in its support for the anti-apartheid, not Russia as such. But no, again, says South Africa's premier *déclassé* politician, Julius Malema. Expressing his desire for a new world order, one freed from US hegemony (a critique not without merit), Malema inveighed against NATO and pledged his support for Russia. And, these voices, astute and unfailingly accurate in their anti-apartheid recollections, go on to argue, Ukraine was part of the Soviet Union, making it six of one (Russia) and half a dozen of the other (Ukraine). Like Ramaphosa, his arch-enemy in South African politics, Malema's view of the world is untroubled by the truth of history. Refusing to distinguish between Russia and the Soviet Union, Ramaphosa's and Malema's is an imperial view of history. So much for having been educated in the anti-apartheid struggle. Ramaphosa's and Malema' is a historically anachronistic view, and a nostalgic one too. One which remembers the Soviet Union's support for anticolonial and the anti-apartheid struggle but, trapped in the past, it remains loyal to a political animal made extinct more than thirty years ago. It is a view of history that continues to find echo chambers in Africa, from dictatorial Mali to expatriates from Sankara's Burkina Faso.[56]

However, what made Malema's pronouncement so odious and offensive, was that it took place at a rally commemorating the Sharpeville Massacre. On March 21st, 1960, disenfranchised South Africans staged a protest against apartheid. The apartheid police shot and killed 69 people, in addition to the 180 who were injured, among them 29 children. Malema chose Sharpeville Day, of all days, to endorse Putin's war. Even if one is so willfully ignorant as to be unable to distinguish the Soviet Union from Russia, shouldn't the historically oppressed throw in their lot with the current victims of an aggression, an attack on a sovereign people born of nostalgia for empire? That is what "any man of sense" would do, not so? But, Ramaphosa, Malema and their South African ilk forget, do they not? Historical amnesia is the most offensive form of violence against historical memory.

However, the truth is less complicated. And not even remotely concerned with history. Ukraine is a minor player in the global economy. Ukraine can offer South Africa, Brazil and India little by way of economic prospect. Russia is a partner in that economic project that seeks to challenge US-European-Chinese economic dominance. "Why, any man of economic sense" would choose Russia over Ukraine, would he not? The road to Indian economic prosperity runs through Moscow and St. Petersburg, through western Siberia, where Russia's greatest oil reserves are to be found. It does not run through Kyiv.

No matter. Exactly what will it take for these BRICS members, at least three of which know what it means to struggle against oppression, to come to their senses? Are they impervious to Ukrainian deaths? To the destruction of Ukrainian cities? What more will it require? "How many roads must a man walk down?" Is it not enough as the world stands on the brink of the largest humanitarian disaster in Europe since World War II?

I am made ashamed by the anti-apartheid slogans of my youth and early adulthood. "An injury to one is an injury to all." How my generation of disenfranchised South Africans, and several before and at least one after, struggled against a racist white minority regime in that cause. It was not only apartheid that we would not endure but fascism in any form, anywhere. We stood with oppressed peoples the world over. Or so I understood the universality of "injury." I was wrong. "An injury to one" is, well, "an injury to one."

Non-aligned, a pivotal influence at Bandung, India, pledged its support for disenfranchised South Africa. "The answer, my friend," has been blown away by the dust, the dust that rises from the rubble, the dust that swirls in the on-going shelling of Ukraine as even monasteries sheltering Ukrainians fleeing the war finds itself bombed. A man must walk down many roads. And he will find, Bob Dylan's man, as he walks, that many of them are threatened by land and by air. A man must walk each road expecting death. The answer assumes, as it must, a haunting, deathly visage. It is an answer that leaves us, as it leaves Telemachus, Odysseus' son, with nothing but "tears and grief" (Ibid). Telemachus shed tears for his long-absent father. South Africans and Indians of a certain generation, Russians of a particular political disposition (those who oppose, those who protest like the Soviet-born Belarussian athlete Aleksander Lesun,[57] those find themselves hapless, too afraid to speak or act; those who have fled, those who wish they could flee, those conscripted against their wishes), it falls to us to grieve for what seems so irrevocably lost. What we have lost is the prospect of solidarity with the other, with those who, within and well beyond national borders, share our commitment to a world made in a just image. Disenfranchised South Africa was greatly aided in its struggle against apartheid by those outside its borders. Disenfranchised South Africa benefited immensely from gifts made to it, made in its name. The nature of the gift is that it breaks the cycle of exchange. Of economic exchange. It gives without the expectation of reciprocation. That is the only gift, as Marcel Mauss' ethnographic work teaches us, worthy of the name "gift."

Is this not an opportunity for the post-apartheid South African government to make a gift, the gift of speaking against Russia's war on the Ukraine, to the Ukrainian people? If such a logic will not take hold, could we not argue that to those whom much is given, of them much is expected? Expected, especially in the moment of historical record. Is that not the common sense of political struggle? Or has the new common sense, "an injury to one is an injury to one," already won out?

If not, are we now to come to the conclusion that it was only the Congress Party, the Congress Party made in Nehru's image which, for all its shortcomings, that stood with disenfranchised South Africa? Tragically, that appears to be the case. Modi's BJP looks inward, and backward, more concerned with disenfranchising its Muslim minority than with injustices beyond its borders. More interested even, as Congress leader Rahul Gandhi says, in spreading "hatred and terror" than addressing the country's economic woes.[58] The commonsense of Hindutva is indifference to all except India's Hindu majority. The commonsense of post-apartheid South Africa is that the accumulation of capital by a black bourgeois minority takes precedence over "injuries" elsewhere. Capital accumulation of the Ramaphosa-variety induces historical amnesia. The logic is irrefutable: it is more lucrative for an ex-trade union leader, turned national leader, to forget than to remember that the world once stood by his people. After all, where is the sense in remembering? What is to be gained from recollecting historical injury, no matter that it is laid bare before you? Much as each of them would refute such a suggestion, at least in relation to their support for Putin, Ramaphosa and Malema are cut from the same ideological and economic cloth. They differ only in their mode of address. The smooth, veteran pol, and the crude nationalist whose ideology always flirts with racist invective.

BLOODYMYR ROMANOV

Still, is it not in the cause of our common collective good that we oppose that which is happening before our very eyes? Is not in our collective interest to do whatever it is we can to prevent what could be an apocalyptic outcome? What will it take for all of us to come to our senses? Significant sectors of the Russian population, who risk a 15-year prison sentence merely by taking to the streets of Russian cities and towns across that country, already expect the worst. Is there not sense enough for us in the lengthy incarcerations these Russians will be made to endure? These protesters risk their lives in saying *Nyet* to Putin.

And so we begin again, out of historical necessity. Again, it seems that we must produce, as if from scratch, a commonsense fitted for our moment. A commonsense that recognizes that there are no innocent global actors. And, because this is true, then all those countries who abstain from condemning Russia should understand that whatever "new world order" they would like to bring into being, there will be costs. China, whose ambitions for global domination is unambiguous, will surely practice a form of international engagement no less ruthless, exploitative and self-interested than the very US-EU axis they wish to displace. The likes of Egypt, Tunisia, India and South Africa, and a host of others, are all hedging their bets, assuming the position of strategic neutrality. Condemning Russia's actions when it is too costly not to, withholding criticism when they think they can get away with it. Strategic neutrality works on the logic that individual nations do not want to get on the wrong side of China. They do not want to anger Russia because if Putin "wins," they want the plausible deniability defense. What the likes of Egypt and South Africa forget is that there is no reason to expect a, say, China-dominated world will be any better for the strategic neutrals. It could, indeed, be worse. Be careful of what you wish for, Julius Malema. Supporting Putin and cozying up to Xi guarantees nothing. Clinging to strategic neutrality, as Navalny has long warned, serves only to embolden rulers given carte blanche by their population.

What Sankara intuited about environmental degradation almost pales in comparison to the global devastation that will follow if Putin chooses to activate the Zaporizhzhia nuclear power plant in southeastern Ukraine. This plant supplies 25% of Ukraine's electricity. It has been in Putin's hands since March 4th, 2022. It is the most powerful nuclear reactor in Europe.

Whether it wants to confront this possibility or not, and the failure to do so would constitute a political failure of catastrophic proportions, Europe itself is now vulnerable to the potential failure—or, at best, abrogation—of the Kremlin's commonsense.

The time for fiddling is now long past over. In any case, in Rome one imagines they forbade fiddling after Nero's indulgences. Instead, today Rome instructs its functionaries to seize yachts and villas. Only Nero and Putin would be disappointed with this sudden turn from frivolity in the face of real disaster. In Rome, we can say, that they are keeping it real. At the very least, the Italians are—or, they briefly were—at the head of that movement determined to strip Russian oligarchs of their European playthings.

David Byrne, the front man of the now-defunct new wave band Talking Heads (1975-1991), offers an instructive counterpoint to the opulence of the Russian oligarchs by recalling for us the striking sparseness of the Pravda offices: "I remember visiting Pravda headquarters in Moscow in the '90s .... In that room there were no decadent touches—which in a power nexus like that was a little surprising. There is almost an absence of power symbols—no marble staircase, giant chandeliers, or even soft leather chairs. Maybe this austerity was meant to be representative of the higher calling being represented, but in this context that pretension coupled with absolute power became all the more chilling."[59] Was it that Pravda so ostentatiously lacked the trappings of power that inspired the Russian oligarchs, with their underground swimming pools in London, their expensively equipped superyachts, their grand mansions in Italy, to tend so blatantly toward excess? All of it so obviously, so garishly, maybe even so desperately *nouveau*?

Marx, we remember, despised the bourgeoisie for their lack of imagination. For their propensity for doing nothing but imitating the ruling classes, their "betters." It would be pathetic, Putin's massive wealth, if the cost wasn't so high for the Russian people. All the oligarchs' wealth makes the Politburo members of old with their well-appointed dachas look like petty thieves. A lack of criminal imagination, really No real appetite for capital accumulation. Hardly an indiscretion at all. And all this, the ostentatious show of wealth, is as much a "chilling," a Czarist, instance of state capture as it is a failure of Russian politics. This Bloodymir Romanov hath wrought.

And much of the blame for what Putin hath wrought rests with the Russian people themselves. Not only that famed older, rural demographic, who rely on state media for their worldview, but Russia's tech-savvy youth, with educated, worldly, liberal and left Russians too. When the anti-Putin Russian intelligentsia sought refuge outside Russia, Navalny determined that there was the absolutely necessity for an oppositional presence. Even if that meant risking being poisoned by Putin's agents. When anti-Putin Russians chose to withdraw from politics, focusing their energies instead on local matters (civil society activism), Navalny insisted on political confrontation as a non-negotiable. Always, of course, at considerable risk. Navalny knows that unless Putin is made to face his antagonists, unless Putin is on the receiving end of political resistance, he will ride roughshod over everyone and he will trample all over democratic institutions. Even removed at a safe distance from the fighting in Ukraine, Putin retreated from public view. Imagine how Putin might cower were he made to face a Russian people united in their opposition to him.

The Russian people are, no matter their rabid ethno-nationalism or their very real fear of state retribution, bear a real responsibility for what is being done to the people of Ukraine, many of whom are, as we said, blood relatives. And, if these Russians are willing to betray their own flesh and blood, there will surely be a historical accounting. As things stand now, the Russian people deserve Putin. They are his enablers. There is blood on their hands. Ukrainian blood. In addition to Cechen and Georgian blood.

If Russians wish to be regarded as members of the global community, then they must resist Putin. They must act out of concern for the deaths of their neighbors. Of their cousins. Of their kinfolk, in short. They must act in the name of something other than their ethno-national selves.

To date, only a small percentage of Russians have shown themselves capable of such an act.

That they have not done so is not for want of a political example.

In refusing a ride from his would-be US protectors, we can say that Zelensky was doing nothing but following Navalny's example.

Difficult to say, but Zelensky may stand second in courage to Navalny. A petty dispute, to be sure. After all, what is the difference between choosing to return sure in the knowledge that physical and psychological harm will certainly follow and deciding to remain when Putin's military has you in its sights?

But no Russian who is either a Putin partisan or remains stubbornly indifferent to the war in Ukraine can ever say that there was not an alternative possibility. Can never say that support for Putin or silence were the only options.

They must instead prepare themselves to face the commonsense truth that Putin partisanship or feigned neutrality was a choice. And that choice has a historical name. Complicity. Complicity in the death of the Ukrainian people. There is enough Russian responsibility to go around.

Staying, and fighting, is a choice that is always available.

ROMAN ABRAMOVICH, CHELSEA FOOTBALL CLUB

In Britain, where we know that London has long been flush with Russian rubles, it took a huge public outcry for Boris Johnson's Tory before British bureaucrats followed the example of their Italian cousins. (Johnson also facilitated a peerage for Evgeny Lebedev, the son of a KGB officer.)[60] To my delight, the sanctions imposed on Russian oligarchs included severe punishment on Roman Abramovich. A Putin intimate, Johnson's government effectively seized ownership of Abramovich's Chelsea Football Club (FC). As a lifelong Liverpool supporter, I've long harbored an intense dislike for all that expropriated (Russian) wealth flowing into Chelsea's coffers.[61]

I can't say I'll be sad to see the end of Chelsea FC, if it comes to that. Chelsea is a west London Tory establishment institution if there ever was one. Liverpool, owned by American billionaire John Henry, isn't exactly free of the machinations of capital, but at least I can say that my club is not in-directly responsible for the death of Ukrainians. And yet, for all that, just denouncing Abramovich, Chelsea and their truly awful fans leaves a bad taste in my mouth. Chelsea fans are today a motley assemblage of the London and international nouveau riche and a bunch of "yobs"—unruly thugs given to physical aggression and verbal abuse, in the English vernacular. (In short, hooligans, louts, vandals, delinquents, always in search of trouble. And where they don't find it, they create it.) Together with Millwall FC, Chelsea fans, celebrated in their famous Shed End, were perhaps the most racist group of English fans in the 1970s and '80s. (Millwall is a club from Bermondsey, southeast London, who play in the second tier of English football. They have an ugly history of racist violence.) And here I speak as a black Liverpool fan, because my club has its own nasty racist history. But we can't, small mercies, hold a candle to Chelsea and certainly not to Millwall.

In addition to their innate west London racism, Chelsea also boasted a proud history of white nationalist gang violence. In fact, an entire mythology of gang violence that sprang up around the club. (The worst of this lot were the notorious "Headhunters," renowned for their extreme violent propensities.) Before Abramovich bought them in 2003, they were, like Brentford FC (beneficiaries now of a new small west London football romanticism, but with their own nasty past), just a small west London club with no history of success of which to speak. Us Liverpool fans have taunted our Chelsea counterparts since about their success. We state it clearly, we Scousers, native-born and long-distance partisans: "You have no history." And now you have a very ugly one. Chelsea bought their success. Like Manchester City, a club owned by an Abu Dhabi conglomerate. Which is to say, Manchester City is the soft power face of the UAE.

SOUNDS LIKE A BILLY JOEL SONG, BUT IT ISN'T: PEP AND EDDIE

> Brenda and Eddie were the popular steadies
> And the king and the queen at the prom
> Riding around with the car top down
> And the radio on
>
> —Billy Joel, "Scenes from an Italian Restaurant."

Pep Guardiola, the Manchester City manager, whom I liked as a player and have tremendous regard for as a manager, is generally a man possessed of good political sense. You can rely on him to be on the right side of things. Not surprising, Pep is a product of Barcelona FC, both as player and massively successful manager. As such, Pep is heir to the venerable tradition that is Barcelona FC anti-fascist past (as well as their present) and Catalonia's historic struggle for the Spanish Republican cause. At the height of the recent struggle for Catalan independence, Guardiola, proudly, wore a Catalan button on the Manchester City sideline.

However, whenever he is quizzed about the politics of the Abu Dhabi conglomerate, Guardiola bristles. As a matter of practice, Guardiola is a thoughtful interview. Deep thinking, competitive, with a mischievous edge. Just watching him, then, impatiently field questions about the source of Manchester City's riches, one knows that, try as he might, articulate as he is, Pep just can't square this political circle. The justness of the Catalan cause is incommensurate with the expropriation of UAE wealth.

So, it makes perfect sense, then, Pep's discomfort. After all, it is the self-same Abu Dhabi rulers who are offering Russian oligarchs refuge for their blood-soiled riches in the UAE who allow Manchester City to spend untold millions on acquiring players. And paying Pep a princely sum in wages. 30 pieces of silver? One wonders. At least, as they say, Pep has a conscience. He can be discomforted.

Not so the Newcastle United manager, Eddie Howe. Quizzed

about the Saudi riches that it is hoped will transform perennial Premier League strugglers Newcastle into the equivalent of Manchester City, Howe dissembled. He knew nothing about politics, or the global financial system, he protested, and he was certainly ignorant of how Saudis came upon such great wealth. Howe pronounced himself "not qualified" to comment on such worldly matters.[62] His job, Howe insists, is to "stick to football." It is impossible here not to suggest that Eddie Howe is the most prominent British graduate of the Laura Ingraham school of political philosophy. Under the guise of political incompetence, Howe was nevertheless taking a leaf from Ingraham's racist playbook. (Howe, I hasten to add, is no racist.)

However, instead of attacking, as Ingraham did when she instructed LeBron James to "shut up and dribble" when James levelled criticisms against the Trump regime, Howe has chosen ignorance and incompetence as a defense.

On the face of it, nothing as offensive as "Shut up and dribble." Howe's is not even a polite request to cease and desist with the questions. Enough already with all this stuff about Saudi blood money, assassinating journalists in Turkey, homophobia, the death penalty. Howe's refusal to address difficult issue is more bland and superficially inoffensive in its cynicism. It's a strategy. Outlast them. Through presenting yourself as manifestly unqualified. Howe hopes that by pleading the fifth, this entire line of questioning will just, somehow, magically, vanish. Howe's learned well from Ingraham. The worst possible thing you can when faced with a political difficulty is not to draw attention to yourself. It's exactly the opposite. Just construct a veil of willful ignorance. It doesn't matter if you're just playing ignorant or if you're really so impervious to the violence being committed by your employers. Our Mr. Howe, unlike Billy Joel's "Eddie," doesn't even have the "radio on." Eddie Howe doesn't do analog technology. Or, digital either.

Instead, Howe's decided to just continue, time after time, question after question, to present himself as not only unschooled in worldly matters, but uneducable on these matters.

It's as though Howe is actually familiar with the "grandfather's curse" in Ralph Ellison's *Invisible Man*. "We'll yes 'em to death and destruction," the dying man says very early on in Ellison's novel. A man of literature, our Eddie Howe?

Hardly. On the contrary. On the basis of his baseless denials, we are left to conclude that Eddie Howe is certifiably illiterate. He does not read because he cannot read. And because he cannot read Howe is "not qualified" to educate himself on the goings-on of his paymasters. No wonder then that Howe turned a deaf ear to the call by Amnesty International to speak out on the atrocities—murdering dissident journalists in Turkey, such as Jamal Khasoggi, for one—being committed in Saudi Arabia.[63]

The weather's abysmal in Newcastle so no one, I imagine, "drives around with the car top down." But how much does the view that is the landscape around St. James' Park, Newcastle's home ground, shield the mind from the specter of 81 executions?[64] Shia terrorists, all, insists the Crown Prince Mohammed bin Salman ("MBS" to his friends in Washington, London, and Ankara, among other places); *al Queda* operatives, surely.[65] You need a whole lot of Newcastle lager, drunk to a Billy Joel soundtrack (not likely), to get that image out of your head, Eddie. Maybe you drink and listen until you develop permanently the kind of amnesia that blots out Saudi atrocity entirely. (No one plays Billy Joel in Newcstle because who'd choose a Long Island crooner when you the likes of Bryan Ferry, Mark Knopfler, and Sting are all native sons?) While Howe continues to plead his ignorance, a new term has been coined to describe Saudi soft power: "blood washing." Nothing soft about power that bathes—washes—itself in the blood of the executed dead. Or, as is the case with "MBS," wears it as a badge of ethno-nationalist, anti-Shia, Wahabi-inspired pride.

All forms of information, from newspaper to all those social media platforms that dispense information so incessantly, are beyond Howe's comprehension. We are also left to conclude that Eddie Howe is hearing deficient. He cannot hear what is being said, all over the place, about not only how Saudi wealth is accrued, at what cost, and at what cost to whom, but the country's policies on women. Howe will not hear about Saudi sponsorship of terror organizations from the Middle East to Africa while also remaining deaf to its homophobia and its fealty to the death penalty. Nor can Howe sign, in either the British or the American system. All forms of communication are beyond his capacities. The only form of communication Howe is capable of is issuing instructions to his players and his coaches. That, and maybe the odd bark at the referee when Howe thinks the official has made a bad call.

We can conclude, however, that Eddie Howe is fully numerate. He can negotiate his contract. He knows how much he wants to be paid. He knows how much Newcastle United can afford to pay for either a player they wish to sign or a player whose contract the club intends to renew. If you can count, who needs to be able to read? Numeracy presents a slight problem, however, because if you can count what do you do when Saudi Arabia puts 81 people to death in a single day?[66] Poor Eddie Howe, he can't win for losing.

Quite a pair they make, Pep and Eddie. And what a ballad is being sung to them in Dubai and Riyadh.

In the service of kings, they are, where every day is "prom" day. If not Billy Joel's "prom" day, then certainly every Friday is big payday for Pep and Eddie. As it is, I hasten to add, for the Liverpool manager, Jurgen Klopp, who brings home a cool £300,000 every week.

BRITTNEY GRINER AND THE WNBA

Speaking of paydays. It is worth remembering that the U.S. athlete now most famously caught up in Russia's war is Brittney Griner, a former WNBA star who played for the Phoenix Mercury. A massively successful player at every level, from high school (entered her senior year as the top-ranked player in the country) to college (at Baylor), from the Mercury to the Olympics (gold medal winner in 2016 and again in 2020). Griner, however, quit the WBNA to move to Russia, where she is now being detained on a trumped-up charge.[67] Since the 2013-14 off-season, Griner, long unhappy with her WNBA salary, has played abroad. In the 2013-14 WBNA off-season Griner played in China, earning $600,000, twelve times her WNBA salary. After her stint in China, Griner joined UMMC Ekaterinburg in the Russian Premier League.

Griner finds herself at the mercy of the Russian authorities, a situation precipitated by the dismal salaries (relative to the salaries in the NBA). Pope-like, caught in a right royal mess of its own making, WNBA officials have been categorical—that is to say, vague—rather than vociferous, as they should be, in their call for Griner's unconditional release. After all, Briner is one of their own, among their best players. However, because the WNBA knows its salary scale is the reason why Briner has to spend her off-seasons in first China then Russia, protesting Griner's detention would work only to shine a critical light on how miserably the league renumerates its players.

Detained by the Russian authorities, made into a bargaining chip by Putin, Brittney Griner is paying the price because the WNBA will not pay her what she deserves.

The WNBA can retreat into generalities all it wants, but all roads will eventually lead back to it. The WNBA's fiscal structure is the reason that Brittney Griner finds herself behind bars.

THOMAS TUCHEL

However, sticking it to Chelsea (and Manchester City; I don't consider Newcastle to belong to the elite in the English Premier League), justified as it is, nevertheless leaves me feeling slightly queasy. On the other hand, maybe I shouldn't waste my good sense on Abramovich and his most expensive plaything. After all, when Chelsea played Norwich City in early March, 2022, the Chelsea fans chanted Abramovich's name.

Hard not to conclude that they deserve each other, Abramovich and the "yobs" who have been weaned on his financial excess. It makes me long for Ol' Blue Eyes, "And now, the end is near ..."

I will say this about Chelsea, however. Their German manager, Thomas Tuchel, has repeatedly asked the club's fans to stop this behavior. I doubt they'll listen. Decency, doing the right thing. That is most definitely not the Chelsea way.

For his part, however, Tuchel can hold his head high. He's been on the right side of this issue from the very beginning. He admitted, when the war began, that football had to take a back seat to the fate of Ukraine. He acknowledged that the world would now be arraigned against Chelsea. He did all this in, if not a shy way, then with a certain sober honesty—probity. Apart from the occasional outburst of frustration, that is. At a press conference about a week into the atrocities he was rather annoyed that reporters would not let go of the issue. What Tuchel failed to understand then is that as long as the war rages, these are the questions that he will be made to answer.

A kind of sympathy for Tuchel, then, because of his near-exemplary conduct. And, what makes Tuchel's commonsense and decency so much more impressive is that he has been left out on a PR island all by himself. It is the Chelsea manager who is the lone voice speaking in Chelsea's name. Every other Chelsea official, every Chelsea player, every former Chelsea player, especially those, such as their "yob-like" and racist former skipper, John Terry, club stalwarts such as Frank Lampard, now managing Liverpool's crosstown neighbors Everton, and the always erudite Graeme le Saux, now an insightful commentator, have not broken their silence on this issue. Everyone but Tuchel has run for cover, never venturing anywhere near a microphone or a camera.

Behavior entirely out of character for the likes of Chelsea's chairman, Bruce Buck, and director, Marina Granovskaia. Neither are what you'd call shrinking violets. At least until now. At least the "yobs" remain loyal, even if it's only to remind everyone, and not only Liverpool fans, just ask Fulham supporters how they feel about this, of why we so despise Chelsea in the first place. As the "yobs" chant "Abramovich," Buck and Granovskaia, are headed for the exit.[68] Quite frankly, I am not sure which is worse. Buck's silence or Granovskaia shopping her CV around. In truth, it feels like Hobson's choice. That is, no choice at all. There is no lesser of two evils here. Meanwhile, on the PR frontline, like William Carlos Williams' "Red wheelbarrow," everything depends on Thomas Tuchel.

In the discourse of English football in the moment of the Ukrainian war, Tuchel's is the only (west London) voice that has emerged as an authentic one. Tuchel's is a voice modulated by humility, inflected by sensitivity to what is happening in Ukraine. As a Liverpool fan, the fan of a club that has long stood as the bastion of working-class radicalism, I can say without hesitation that I admire Thomas Tuchel.[69] I have no time for Chelsea, but Tuchel, he has risen to the occasion. Whatever regrets he may or may not have about the position he finds himself in, he's kept them to himself. Good, honest, lad, as they say. A real Sinatra boy he is: "I faced it all/And I stood tall." Nonetheless, this a rough time to be forced to do it your way.

I have every regard for the ways in which Tuchel expresses, under very difficult circumstances, an authentic concern for how it is we are in the world. What it is he, as a human being, as a football manager caught in poisonous web not of his own making, stands for. And, what he stands against. Speaking in deliberate tones, embodying a modesty that suggests a man wrestling with his darker angels while determined to simultaneously pay heed to his better ones, Tuchel, much as he was until just a few short days ago in the pay of Abramovich, is against chanting the name of a Putin fellow-traveler. It is commonsense to Tuchel what the "Abramovich" chant signifies. To a significant Chelsea constituency (the Chelsea Confederacy?), allegiance to Abramovich's capital and the glory it has secured the club since Abramovich first took ownership in 2003, is all that matters.

Under such conflicted conditions, authenticity wages an uphill battle. Would not commonsense dictate that, in this moment the inauthentic bow to the authentic? Maybe no more pro-Abramovich chants? In its stead, a banner that reads, "In Tuchel We Trust?" as though you were Manchester United's poor west London cousins? (Remember when Manchester United fans proclaimed, "In Moyes We Trust?" A cruel joke to which the Mancs were blind. But here's the opportunity, Chelski fans, to turn that notion to good.) I'm not suggesting that you Chelsea fans take a moral lesson from a Liverpool partisan. Far be it from me to do that. I've got my own demons which I might never be able to excise. Liverpool's ugly, racist past, about which I've written with as much complexity as I can muster, will do that to you. I still tie myself in knots about my early Liverpool fandom, partisan that I am. "Regrets, I've had a few." There are some things that you just don't forget. Maybe you don't even forgive yourself for them. Writing a love letter to your club, as I have, does not rise to the level of absolution. And it may be absolution from my own past, for too long unexamined, that I write in search of; that may be why I wrote *Long Distance Love*.

Still and all, you west London lot, I am, at best, indifferent to you. However, I feel for your manager. There is no *schadenfreude* for me so far as Tuchel goes.

I quite frankly don't think you appreciate the difficult task he has been assigned. You're an unthinking bunch if there ever was one. Throw Tuchel a bone. Just stop the chants. Silence is all that is required. The rest of the world would be quite justified in demanding that you condemn Abramovich. He still hasn't spoken out against Putin's war against Ukraine. The entire non-Chelsea universe asks only that you not offend the people of Ukraine for any longer than you already have. Ukrainians are dying. Mothers, newborn children, old folks, and soldiers too; young women are being raped. What is it with you that it appears that even so relatively small a request, "Say Nothing," is too much to expect of the likes of you? If you had a history, perhaps you'd know what this moment so obviously needs. For your troubles, you're now going into the history books as the beneficiaries of corrupt, bloody money. However, since you're Chelsea fans, you probably think it was all worth it. Congrats.

If that is not enough, try to recall a former Chelsea player. Andrei Shevchenko. A Ukrainian. A striker with a lethal touch. On the football field. A quiet, thoughtful man off the field. Is he not worthy of your contemplation, if not your sympathy? Is there no room for the authentic in your boisterous inauthenticity? If you're not careful, Chelsea, you could become the Millwall FC of Europe. A team playing in the second tier of English football, Millwall fans, notoriously racist and violent, are a defiant bunch. Their motto, overwritten pathos, is "No one likes us; we don't care." Oh, but they do care, they care very much, don't they? That's why they remind us of their not being liked all the time.

The Chelsea chanters, "yobs," "headhunters," would be well advised to remember that Tuchel is not hostile to them. Although, to my mind, he should be. However, Tuchel's got burden enough to bear. So, you Chelski fans, try to care. For Tuchel's sake. While you still have a club. Before they turn your posh ground, Stamford Bridge, into a parking lot. If you can't stop your chants, maybe it's better if you just take yourselves off to Millwall.

Take away the success you've enjoyed under Abramovich, 17 trophies, that's quite a haul, and there's no distinguishing Chelsea fans from their Millwall cousins. Unless you can get some commonsense, but quickly, a new chant might erupt on football grounds all over England and Europe. You'll recognize it immediately: "We don't like you because you don't care."

In this unprecedented moment, Thomas Tuchel is the finest "Servant" Chelsea could have. He is also the "Servant" that they are showing themselves to be totally unworthy of.

BLUE AND YELLOW

When I first became a Liverpool fan more than fifty years ago, Chelsea's colors were blue and yellow. Yes, the colors of the Ukrainian flag. Thomas Tuchel is the only person in the entirety of Chelsea FC who has, in a strange historical irony, revived that tradition. Tuchel, in my imagination, has donned those now abandoned colors, blue shorts, yellow jersey fringed with blue, in order to declare fidelity to a larger cause. Tuchel *über alles*. Tuchel is the well-traveled German manager (with stints in his native Germany, France, England) who is, despite considerable odds, determined to symbolically connect west London to Kyiv. If we allow ourselves a moment of hubris here, we can say that Tuchel is symbolically undoing Brexit.

In this way, Tuchel is of a (small) piece with Zelensky. That is because, in making Europe universally vulnerable to nuclear disaster, Putin may have assigned to a Slavic Jew the unenviable but heroic and maybe even the necessary task of reconstituting Europe. Of remaking Europe in such a way as Europe never knew itself. Europe, we can now confidently say, begins in Crimea and then wends its way through Kyiv and Lviv, toward Poland, Hungary, and Romania. More precisely, it begins in Zaporizhzhia. We can only hope that Zaporizhzhia is not where Europe ends.

A Europe remade from and by its eastern outpost. It is hoped that this will be the new commonsense of Europe. We will turn our attention to the reconstitution of Europe shortly, but for now we are concerned with one of the qualities that constitute probity.

THE HUMILITY OF THE PLEA

As a figure of probity, Zelensky knows that Ukraine cannot, brave as the Ukrainians have proven to be, do without. "I need." A plea for help, a plea made to Paris, London, Seoul and many places in between. A pressing situation. Ukrainians do not have the resources, military ("ammunition"), to undertake this battle on their own. "I need' is the authentic language of authenticity. Just as "what it is that you need" repeats—codes, substantiates—the language of authenticity. The cheeky complement to "need" is, as argued earlier, the unapologetic reprimand phrased as an indictment—is Russia in charge of NATO?

"I need" reverberates with the sting of a bitter truth. Ukraine cannot fight this battle on its own. As such, "I need," is made into a statement of humility. To not be too proud to ask for help. And to ask repeatedly, if necessary; everywhere it is you go, you ask for what it is you need. To remind those whom you are asking of what it is that is at stake. Reminding them of your precarity. Reminding them that your future depends on what it is they do now. Reminding them of the cost of their failure to help. Not to be above embarrassing those whom you are asking. (Again, the indictment.) Whatever it takes to make your sympathizers do the right thing. No one likes to beg. But needs must. That is the bedrock of political—and even revolutionary—commonsense. The revolutionary leader's decisions, all his actions, must emerge out of the commonsense of the people. In so doing, the leader and the people are one, united in their thinking, collective in their commitment to their shared objective, no matter the difficulties they confront, no matter the circumscription of their choices, no matter the harshness of the conditions they face. "Keeping it real."

Men make history under conditions not of their choosing, is how Karl Marx so sagely phrased this political reality one hundred and eighty years ago in his essay "The Eighteenth Brumaire of Louis Bonaparte." Maybe the most humorous essay in that substantial body of work that is Marx's oeuvre. Marx has a jolly old time making fun of the younger Bonaparte, Napoleon's inept and grandiloquent nephew. Better to be short of stature but lofty of ambition than a bag of hot air, is sort of Marx's verdict. Commonsense is nothing but the good sense to do what it is you know you need to do. And not to linger over doing it. Not to procrastinate. The moment demands. But neither is the demand the moment a license to act hastily or to make poor decisions. Above all, the commonsense of the authentic stipulates the necessity of acting with probity.

In his urgent humility, which is grounded in an unerring honesty, Zelensky figures at once as the epic hero willing to risk his life and that of his family, and as mere spokesperson for the cause of his people. Volodymyr Zelensky cast as the messenger made by history. The work of asking the outside world for help has fallen to him. In quick succession Zelensky goes from Ukrainian Spartacus to national leader in need. Zelensky doesn't care that he needs. It is precisely that he doesn't care that makes him authentic. Zelensky is both epic hero and embattled president. The authenticity of his speech prohibits any daylight between these two positions. The epic hero is the pleading president. Only, we might speculate, authenticity allows for the singularity of such a duality.

DIRECT SPEECH

Volodymyr Zelensky, in his address to the world, in his determination to stay and fight, became, in precisely that moment, the very incarnation of authenticity. His fellow-Ukrainians, as well as much of the world beyond its borders, responded to his words, "I don't need a ride," as an article of truth. A commonsense pronouncement that raises the prospect of international repercussions. An article of truth that could be the prelude to a world war. In our social media age, it is accurate to say that Zelensky's is not, technologically speaking, a direct address. It is mediated by social media, hence the rapid-fire creation of memes honoring his address. Ours is the world of hyper-temporality. Everything moves at the speed of information, and information moves very quickly. And it disseminates itself across all the world. Zelensky, however, seems able to simultaneously overcome mediation and to utilize it. Mediation always opens the possibility for mis- or re-representation and mis- or re-representation has within its capacity the power to frame, distort or do outright violence to the message.

Zelensky overcomes, or negates, mediation by making his television interviews or conducting his social media appearance without any performative apparatus. Of course, every self-presentation is a performance, but the authentic address relies keenly on simplicity of address. That is its virtue. There is nothing technical or bureaucratic in how Zelensky speaks. His language is pared to its essentials. Think FDR's fireside chats, except that you can see the speaker, watch his facial expressions, note the changes in his tone, attend to his every cadence. The effect of all of this is in fact *direct address*. That is, you feel as though Zelensky is speaking directly to you. You are his audience of one, no matter that you watch him speak in a crowded room or on your smartphone with a bunch of friends. That is, his ability to speak directly to you, at the same time, of course, as he is speaking to possibly millions of other people at exactly the same moment. Direct address has the effect of "eradicating" the mediation that is the very stuff of the medium. It's the message that Zelensky makes count. The medium is, well, incidental. That is, the medium, is what makes the address possible in the first place. But it is still only the medium. Intimacy. A personal connection. What we as a viewing public as sometimes quick to dismiss as artificial, as constructed, as worthy of suspicion. We're not wrong in our skepticism, of course, but Zelensky is able to reach us because he appears to have already liquidated mediation. It is just you, the viewer, probably a rapt audience, and him. In place of the patrician FDR's well-kept hearth, what Zelensky offers is infinitely more real. He is a leader, literally, under fire. You can, as it were, hear the bombs being dropped, you can watch Russian tanks firing on Ukrainian buildings, homes, offices, hospitals, schools. There is every chance you'll see buildings being set alight or watch a Russian aircraft falling from the sky.

This is as real as it gets. Its mediated. And yet its anything but. You can picture FDR in a three-piece suit. But you can see Zelensky in his trademark green T-shirt. "Churchill in a T-shirt," the Brits murmured appreciatively after watching him wow all and sundry in their normally boisterous House of Commons. Zelensky has the effect of making it real. What you see is what you get. In a world chock full of artifice, living in the time of rapid communication, Zelensky at work—addressing the world—has the effect of making us appreciate the value of technology and hyper-temporality, while at the same time making us slow down. Slow down so that we can fully absorb his message—that we can begin to process his message. He is speaking to us. He is asking for our help. He is laying bare to us the world as it is. The world as he does not want it to be. Through his direct address, Zelensky is conscripting us into the battle to save Europe. For him, for his people, but also for us. For all of us.

Obviating and exploiting mediation is how, to anticipate the issue that next section takes up, the "Zelensky Method" works. Works for Zelensky, works on us, works in the world through us. No wonder that Colbert, who once played the letter "Z" on *Sesame Street* declared it off limits to Putin. In any case, as Colbert, always alert to ironies of every kind, pointed out, there is no letter "Z" in the Cyrillic alphabet. If there is no such letter in Putin's native tongue, what on earth are all those "Zs" doing on Russian tanks? Is Putin asleep at the wheel? Catching some "Zs" when he should be brushing up on his knowledge of his own alphabet? Or, is it all just an accident? Someone marked their tank with a "Z," and then everyone else in the battalion followed suit? And now you can't walk a block in Moscow or St. Petersburg without a "Z" assaulting your sightline because the arbitrary has become the special operation norm. Is that a meme? All those "Zs," courtesy of a carefully orchestrated campaign coordinated by the Kremlin. *Post ipso facto,* of course.

ON METHODS. THREE, IN FACT

In his opening monologue on his March 10th, 2022, edition of "The Late Show," Colbert was, as we know, punning on the Michael Douglas Netflix show, the "Kominsky Method." In this Netflix series, Douglas plays Sandy Kominsky, a washed-up, aging-faster-than-he-can-believe actor, a geriatric, over-the-hill Lothario who won't give up the ghost. An actor, who, like any artist who can no longer do, is left with the only option available to him: he must teach. Kominsky's grumpy agent has given up on him. The agent, Norman Newlander, in a star turn by Alan Arkin, can't quite bring himself to tell his client that the gig is up—so Sandy and Norman's friendship survives. (In fairness to Norman, however, even when he tries to tell Sandy's that it's over, he won't listen.). The upshot of this sorry state of affairs is that Kominsky, still hoping for one last hurrah, is left to teach a rough assemblage of untalented never-will-bees. And teach he does.

Teaching students his way, the Kominsky Method, is his last chance to recount to a very small, and very captive, audience, his halcyon days in Hollywood. Kominsky teaches, but to little effect. Certainly, to no good effect. It's a hopeless situation. Kominsky can't land an acting gig and so he's opened this acting studio where he deigns to teach. His charges are worse off. They're hardly ever going to get an audition, and they're almost certainly never going to get a call back.

Unlike the "Kominsky Method," where we find a studio on the verge of insolvency, Hollywood's calling Kyiv for the movie rights to the "Zelensky Method." It's definitely a going concern, the "Zelensky Method." It could even be a franchise. One can already see Steve Carell in the leading role. After saving Ukraine, the sequel installs Carell to lead the EU for the foreseeable future. Well and truly bested by Zelensky, Boris Johnson, but not Nigel Farage, asks for a redo on that Brexit vote.

No need to hold off on who might play Putin. It's a role tailor made for Jon Voigt. His and Putin's politics align perfectly. Same charming disposition.

However, if the "Zelensky Method" already has Hollywood blockbuster written all over it, one hopes that it will be followed, in double-quick time, by either an independent docudrama or, better still, a prequel. The "Karensky Method," in which the second-to-last White Russian leader, Alexander Karensky, him of Stanford University Hoover Institute fame, is resurrected to record Putin's last days in power. In the "Karensky Method," we find Putin living in splendiferous exile in any one of these recognizable locations. In addition to having the pick of his *SUI nouveau* cities, Putin will have to decide amongst Beijing, Belgrade (although, to be fair, the Serbs are having serious second thoughts; and, is there really enough oxygen in the city for both Putin and Djokovic?), Rio, Johannesburg (Cape Town's beautiful but too far from the economic action), and New Delhi (Mumbai's India's cultural and economic hub but it really is too crowded for Putin's taste).

Of course, the opportunity to make the "Karensky Method" depends entirely on a repeat of October 1917.

It will require a figure of Leninist proportions to lead a revolution that forces Putin out, into exile. Swept into the dustbin of history along with Putin will be every last vestige of the repressive state apparatuses that Czar Vlad so deliberately assembled over the last twenty-three years. There is no need for anyone to parse Lenin's most famous inquiry, "What is to be done?" We know what must be done. The oligarchs must be held to account. Their ill-gotten gains must be returned to the Russian people. Ukraine must be rebuilt, with Russian money. A Marshall Plan for Ukraine, sponsored by Russia and, for good measure, overseen by a reputable international body so that post-Putin Russia can be held accountable. Ukrainian infrastructure must be rebuilt. In many cases, with hospitals, schools, even places of worship, this rebuilding will have to be done from the ground up. Reparations must be made to the Ukrainian people, beginning with compensation for survivors of the hundreds of thousands of victims, for the orphaned children, for the interrupted education, for the trauma endured by all Ukrainians.

THERE ARE NO WORTHY VICTIMS

The world is rightly outraged when Putin's forces bomb a theatre in Mariupol housing those fleeing from the war, a theatre marked, clearly, in Russian, "Children (дети)."[70] Women, children, maternity hospitals, orphans, the elderly, the infirm, the violence done to those who fall into these categories spark the greatest condemnation. It angers us more because we understand these to be the most vulnerable. And so they undoubtedly are. However, the effect of recognizing, say, children and the elderly, as special categories of victims—categorization not begun with Putin's war—is that every other category of the dead, the injured or the mutilated are thereby diminished. The victims of war are, no matter our good intentions, divided into "worthy" and "unworthy."

Intentionally, or not, we reserve a special sympathy, a higher level of outrage, we can summon up a fiercer condemnation for the old and the infirm cast hapless into the world by Putin's bombs or the terrified children seeking shelter in a Mariupol theatre. In so doing, we make of the other victims, unwittingly, the soldiers, the men and women who staff the barricades in Kyiv or Lyiv, the middle-aged men and women determined to carry on with life on their farms or in their offices, a constituency, if not "unworthy," then something perilously close to it. Whether we intend to or not, through implicit comparison we make their deaths, their injuries, their mutilations, their traumas, less worthy. Not undeserving of our support for the horrors they have endured, but we are more likely to reduce them to the statistical. They "merely" number among the dead. They are not the public face of suffering. Zelensky awards, them, posthumously, medals.

And what of the dead Russian soldiers? How many unwilling conscripts in their ranks?

If we are to rethink how it is we want to be in the world, then we could do worse than insist upon the "worthiness" of all the victims. A soldier's death is a death. Not one the soldier deserved. He is as much a victim as every other dead Ukrainian. It may be that our better angels are more given to mourning for those we deem "deserving." But that leaves us only with the dialectical outcome that some are, implicitly, "undeserving."

In resisting Putin, we must reconsider who it is we deem worthy of Russian violence. In condemning Russian aggression in its entirety, we might insist that we mourn all deaths, if not equally, then certainly with the intention of creating greater equality among the dead. That some are victims appalls us more. We might want to make that assumption, that visceral response, a matter for rethinking.

Untitled by Ilya Kabakov, 2016. Watercolor, color pencils,
black ink on paper. 57 x 40 cm. Copyright: Ilya & Emilia Kabakov.
Courtesy of Ilya & Emilia Kabakov.

AUTHENTIC REVOLUTIONARY

An authentic revolutionary would, in addition to repairing the massive structural damage done to Ukraine, also insist that Ukraine denuclearize. If the world survives this Putinesque horror, an open question *at the time of writing*, then one of the first things that needs attending to is removing from the planet entirely all possibilities of terror deriving from nuclear, chemical and biological weapons. Ours is a dire situation. The threat of the planet being destroyed because of the whims of a single agent, one trained in the finer points of Soviet spy craft, no less, should compel us all to organize the life of the planet in a radically different way. A way that will no longer tolerate the threat of planetary destruction.

We're not hard-pressed for examples of such an imaginary at all. We could do worse than take our cues from the Aldermaston marches, that anti-nuclear movement of the 1950s. Revised and updated for our moment but infused with the same spirit. Averting destruction on the order of Hiroshima, Nagasaki and, since this is Ukraine we're talking about, Chernobyl.

In the most perverse of ironies, Vladimir Putin might be the catalyst that makes it clear to us that we are duty-bound to begin the work of saving ourselves from our worst selves. Putin, the oligarchs, the all-too compliant Russian polis that stood by, with only the occasional act of resistance, while setting us on the path to this horrific moment, they must be made into a negative theology. *Bilse ni.* (*більше ні*). *No mas. Nunca mas.*

It is imperative that we oppose Putin, bring an end to his reign of terror. However, that is by no means enough.

TAKING A CUE FROM "TALKING HEADS"

Carpe diem. We must seize this moment to begin the work of determining how to live differently. To live differently in relation to each other, beginning with how we structure our relations with our neighbors. We must commit to living in such a way that the prospect of planetary devastation is not our primary existential concern. As Byrne writes in his advocacy for making cities the world over better for human habitation, much of which derives from Byrne's experience as an urban cyclist, "life can be good—not only good, it can be better than most of us can imagine" (Byrne, 41).

The Talking Heads' remaking of Antonio Gramsci's famous maxim: pessimism of the intellect, optimism of the will. A cool kid from the Baltimore suburbs (born in Scotland) who fled those self-same suburbs (for New York, of course), Byrne, it should be noted, is writing in his *Bicycle Diaries*, his nod to Ché, about the experience of riding through rustbelt cities such as Detroit and Pittsburgh, U.S. cities determined to make for themselves a new mode of living in the aftermath of economic collapse and indifference from the feder -al government. Detroit and Pittsburgh, much like Syracuse and Rochester (NY), Erie (PA) and Cleveland (OH), are cities, as we well know, that have endured all manner of upheaval and devastation, cities left to fend for themselves in no small measure because they're historically black majority cities. Black populations abandoned to find their way to something other than the kind of structural neglect to which they have been condemned. Told to fend for themselves.

Borrowing from the Baltimore Gramsci, we should insist, in our determination to make our world anew even as Putin is hell-bent on destroying it, that this is no mere pie-in-the-sky idealism. It is, instead, a further exploration of what it would take to make of our world a utopia. That is, livable. Livable for all. Not only denuclearized (understood as a composite for the banning all forms of non-conventional warfare), but, demilitarized (banning all forms of conventional warfare). Not only refusing to buy any more Russian oil, but, figuring out how to accelerate the timeline by which we can live in a fossil-free world.[71]

How we can put an end to humanity's seemingly unending capacity to put all life on the planet at risk. How we can do away with the rhetoric of "energy independence," that hoary old right-wing chestnut, just dripping with nationalist invective and insecurity, and instead build toward a shared reliance on—and universally shared access to—clean energy.

This is not to propose that we thank Putin. *Nyet.* Far from it. But, if *he* is to be the pivotal figure in our doctrine of negative theology, then this is certainly a call to ensure that we abandon the path we're on. The path every national unit is on, as well as the path that we're on globally.

OPPOSITION BEGINS AT HOME

One is cheered by a Russian officer, Major Viktor Blyudin. Together with five members of his unit, Major Blyudin surrendered to Ukrainian civilians "near the town of Sribne in the southern part of Chernihiv oblast."[72] Having heard of the bad end to which nearby Russian troops had come, the six soldiers decided to surrender, and not only because they decided that discretion was the better part of valor. Notwithstanding an understandable skepticism about their motives, the Russians were after all egged on by filming locals to declare their opposition to Putin, the Major and is unit appeared only to happy to oblige. The nicest thing they had to say about Putin was calling him a "scumbag." They seemed much more vociferous about declaring their putative leader a "d-ckhead."

Major Blyudski and his comrades, the Russian journalist Marina Ovsyannikova ("No War," talk about crashing a party, spectacularly),[73] the thousands of protesters all across Russia. Something to hold onto. Encouraging, demanding that more Russians break ranks with the Kremlin. According to Putin all opposed to him are nothing but "scum" (sense a theme developing here), fifth columnists, traitors to the Russian people. Each of these figures, each in their own way, is insistent: *Bilse ni. No mas.* *"Bolsze net (больше нет)"* is what Navalny would have his compatriots say, loudly, repeatedly. Navalny and Zelensky must loom large in the thinking of the "fifth columnists," a designation that should be worn with pride. But what is happening in terms of domestic opposition to Putin *at the time of writing* is not enough. The necessary next step is to intensify that refusal, to magnify that opposition to the Kremlin, to grow those numbers of protesters exponentially. All across the vast landmass that is Russia, across all of its 13 time zones, from Siberia to Sochi, from Moscow to Vladivostok. What is necessary now is that it becomes possible to say what needs to be said. *Bolsze net. Nunca mas.* No more victims of war. *Basta.* _Dostatochno (достаточно)._

GOVERNOR KIM

While the Russian forces seem low on morale and unconvinced about the rationale for invading their neighbors, the Ukrainians seem buoyed at every turn by not only Zelensky, but regional leaders such as Vitaly Kim. As the governor of Mykolaiv Oblast now turned military commander, Kim rallies his populace every day. Via social media, Kim prepares his citizenry for what's to come in the morning. Last thing at night, he either prepares them for what kind of assault they should expect until daybreak or he promises them a good night's rest. In "Kim We Trust," is the motto by which citizens of Mykolaiv Oblast live. The motto by which the Ukrainians in Kim's Oblast pronounce themselves prepared to battle Russians, street-by-street, if necessary, until the death. Like Major Blyudin, Kim too, has a taste for the invective, even though it is sometimes not more than taunting the enemy with a "'Hello, Russian stupid boys.'"[74]

More than a century after the last of the war poets, Rupert Owen, Rupert Brooke, met their grisly end, Owen's haunting title, "Dulce et Decorum Est," "It is good and noble to die for one's country," stands stripped of its bitter irony. Let us say, cautiously, "It is good and noble to die for Ukraine." All the while reminding ourselves that "Dulce et Decorum Est" must still stand as a cautionary tale. All the while knowing that Owen is urging us to never let the facticity of ethno-nationalism out of our sight.

Read against the backdrop of the battle for survival being waged in Kyiv, Lviv, and Sribne, patriotism, Ukrainian-style, finds itself infused with the kind of truth that can sustain a people militarily overmatched but fierce of heart and obstinate in their resistance to Putin. Is it in the actions of Zelensky, Kim and the Ukrainian people that Owen's well-founded critique of the senselessness of war meets its end? However temporary? For a moment, even? As a violence fueled by imperial nostalgia brings untold hardship to an entire nation, how could we not acknowledge the rousing of a national spirit? Mindful, as we should always be, of the atrocities that are all too often committed in the name of the nation. To pay heed to Owen even as we are awestruck by how it is Ukrainians fight for their todays. Tomorrow, after all, will likely, if they are lucky, be witness to another day of struggle.

We can make this provisional Ukrainian patriotism part of, an addendum to, a codicil of, but, whatever we do, let's make sure that it figures prominently in the Zelensky Doctrine. That Doctrine in which we reduce Putin to the briefest footnote. The Doctrine that reveals, clearly, how we have moved determinedly toward a new method according to which we want to live. A world as intolerant of Putin, or Putin-like figures (Trump, Bolsanaro, Orban, Ramaphosa, Modi, to name but the most obvious culprits), as it is unwilling to tolerate *SUI nouveau* accomodationism and expedience. Are they not latter-day Neville Chamberlains, those who pretend (Neftali Bennet, Emmanuel Macron, Sisi, each in his own way) to want end to Putin's war against civilians but do not declare themselves publicly? Are they not paying attention to the "Zelensky Method?"

They are worse than latter-day Chamberlains, but a limp foil for Zelensky's Churchill. Are we to take comfort that they are not waving about worthless bits of paper, claiming to have secured peace for Europe? Prime ministers, autocrats, it is they who make no apology for their dalliance with Putin. Instead, it is they who shamelessly avail themselves of the opportunity to use the moment to fill their nation's coffins. In this category we reserve a special place for the likes of Mohammed bin Salman and Mohammed bin Rashid al Maktoum.[75]

That would really be "keeping it real." But only if we understand the end of Putin as our beginning and not our end.

MAKING COMMON CAUSE

Speaking mainly through an interpreter in his address to the U.S. Joint Houses of Congress a week after he delivered his message to the House of Commons, Zelensky was more explicit in delineating what bound his nation to that of his audience—or, those of his audiences: "Ladies and gentlemen, friends, Americans, in your great history, you have pages that would allow you to understand Ukrainians, understand us now when we need you, right now."[76] Our experience is of the moment, but it is not unique: "in your great history," again, a slightly flattering touch, but, permissible under the circumstances, "you have pages that would allow you to understand Ukrainians." It is "understanding" of such an order, one that stands against tyranny and a bloody imperial nostalgia, that at once needs no translation while simultaneously demanding precisely that.

The Ukrainian situation is explicable to you, Americans, but it nevertheless demands that I, Zelensky, make clear to you what it is I need you to understand. Zelensky needs Americans to "understand" what it is they must do, how they must act, if they are to demonstrate their comprehension of what Russia is doing to Ukraine. To give substance to their "understanding," America must react in the terms of that "understanding." It must give political form and military content to that which Zelensky is presenting as the shared "understanding" of resisting illegitimate violence. We will turn our attention to what is needed shortly, but for now it matters that we acknowledge how that which derives from shared "understanding" draws the self, one sovereign nation, not only close to another, sovereign nation, but, almost literally, into that self. And here that forbidding phrase, "to be drawn into war," resonates. How it is possible to enact responsibility without being drawn into? What is responsibility without full "understanding?"

TO MAKE LANGUAGE BEAR ITS TRUTH

Of course, the need to make language bear its truth and to make that truth evident, the imperative to make interpretation superfluous, all stems from historical urgency. The logic of the "Zelensky Method" is driven by time. There is no time to waste. Interpretation is indulgence.

At the time of writing, Hitler's birthday, Zelensky speaks in precisely the register of existential urgency. Taking to social media, #ArmUkraineNow,[77] Zelensky implores people the world over to insist that their governments provide military support for Ukraine.

There is a resistance to be mounted, a resistance that must be sustained. There is a desperate need for aid and assistance of all manner of things. Food, water, shelter, military supplies—anti-aircraft artillery, bullets, weapons, and, yes, Zelensky even made an appeal for a Ukrainian sniper. "Wali," the sniper, a member of the Canadian armed forces, answered the call.[78] It is said that when "Wali's" on his game, 40 kills a day is possible. (On March 5th or 6th, the Russian general Sukhovetsky was reputedly killed by a Ukrainian sniper.) If anyone knows anything about the deadliness of Ukrainian snipers, it's the Russians. After all, the most successful, if that is the correct term, sniper that the Soviet Union ever had was Lyudmila Pavlichenko (1916-1974), a Ukrainian woman who is credited with 309 kills. "Wali" has been set a steep target. Meanwhile, Ukraine claims to have captured the famous Russian sniper, "Bagira," a former nun turned deadly shot.[79]

The high moment of the "Zelensky Method," however, was not an address to his country. It was his address to the British House of Commons. How he knew that that normally uproarious body would thrill to him. How well he anticipated what they would need to hear. How he presented the greatest oratorical moment in modern British parliamentary history to them, for their consumption. How he knew, with uncanny instinct, what was dearest to them. Even if they had forgotten that long ago moment of direct address. But what the

House of Commons had not forgotten was how one of their own had stirred them to a grand resistance.

"CHURCHILL IN A T-SHIRT"

In his address to the House of Commons, it seems that Zelensky knew the spirit of that institution, in a moment of international crisis, when European democracy was under its gravest threat yet, better than the current members of parliament themselves. Schoolchildren of a certain generation in Britain and its erstwhile colonies know the address well. Even if those schoolchildren do not remember the exact words, or the exact order of the words, they have imbibed its stirring spirit. A memorable date it is in history, June 4th. It was on that date in 1940 when Churchill addressed a Britain that, with the Axis powers in the ascendancy, with France already under a Vichy government, stood on the brink of disaster. It is also the same date that, 49 years later, a lone man stood in front of Chinese military tank in Tiananmen Square, anointing the date with its name—Tiananmen Square Day. With a gravitas unmatched, Churchill sallied forth:

> "I have, myself, full confidence that if all do their duty, if nothing is neglected, and if the best arrangements are made, as they are being made, we shall prove ourselves once again able to defend our Island home, to ride out the storm of war, and to outlive the menace of tyranny, if necessary for years, if necessary alone."[80]

It is precisely the possibility of having to "outlive the menace of tyranny," out of historical "necessity," "alone," that Zelensky is hell bent on avoiding. Churchill, of course, faced considerable difficulties in the moment of his speaking. He was, it is arguable, not addressing a nation so under siege, a people that the enemy wants to extinguish from history to the extent that Zelensky finds himself. Small comfort, but Churchill at least had allies who had been defeated and occupied but were now mounting a famous resistance. Zelensky stands very much alone. Much as the Russian forces had the advantage of surprise, an advantage that they have in fact been unable to exploit, for their part the Ukrainian military do not seem to have made the "best arrangements" possible. Arrangements, which, had they been made, would have provided Ukraine with a better defense.

Whatever "confidence" Zelensky has in his people derives from, symbolically, the public determination evinced by the likes of him and Kim. Of course, the Ukrainian people have more than stepped up to do their "duty." And they continue to do so. And the Ukrainians are clearly motivated to defend their "home." Bravely. In Odessa, a factory owner in his 50s is learning the intricacies of warfare, locals are preparing, à la Normandy, to defend themselves against an amphibious Russian attack. Alongside the newly enlisted men, the women of Odessa are familiarizing themselves with military hardware. Literally a case of all-(Ukrainian)-hands-on-deck.[81]

The story is the same across the length and breadth of Ukraine. Everywhere in the country there are communities mounting defenses such as these. Much more bravely than anyone, including Zelensky and Putin, each in their own, expected. Called upon to fight off invaders, especially invaders determined to wipe an entire people off the face of the earth, the love of motherland, or fatherland, if you prefer, can raise a people to heights that cannot be measured in terms of military resources. Like all those Britons who commandeered every seaworthy vessel to hand to ensure the safety of their troops, stranded in France. They surely could not have known the effect of every individual effort. They were doing nothing but the duty to which Churchill had called them.

For purely military reasons, however, the situation that Zelensky faces has the feel of a greater portentousness. Not least of all because there is no reason for anyone to have confidence that Putin will not resort to biological, chemical, or nuclear warfare. Against this there is nothing in the Ukrainian defense arsenal that can protect the Ukrainian people against such an attack. Hence Zelensky's turn to hyperbolic conspiracy theory—Russia's in charge of NATO. Hence #ArmUkraineNow.

In place of the high-end military technology required to fend off such a disaster, Zelensky, intensely aware of his audience and the rhetoric that would strike at them most directly, did the predictable.

He channeled his inner-Churchill, newly discovered, admittedly, but a persona and a message he knew would resonate with his audience.

Colonialist to the end, this is nonetheless the apogee of Churchillian poetry. Resolute without ignoring the magnitude of the task that awaited Britain. Isolated in the wake of the Axis powers' defeat of France, this is Churchill rousing the British bulldog. Realistic about the cost that Britain may defer, and not unwilling to present the specter of defeat, Churchill nevertheless places his faith in Imperial loyalty. The colonized will rise to the occasion and give their all for Mother England:

> *We shall go on to the end*, we shall fight in France,
>
> we shall fight on the seas and oceans,
>
> we shall fight with growing confidence and growing
>
> strength in the air, we shall defend our Island, whatever
>
> the cost may be,
>
> we shall fight on the beaches,
>
> we shall fight on the landing grounds,
>
> we shall fight in the fields and in the streets,
>
> we shall fight in the hills;
>
> we shall never surrender, and even if, which I do not for a
>
> moment believe, this Island or a large part of it were sub-
>
> jugated and starving, then our Empire beyond the seas,
>
> armed and guarded by the British Fleet, would carry on
>
> the struggle, until, in God's good time, the New World,
>
> with all its power and might, steps forth to the rescue
>
> and the liberation of *the old.*[82]

Stirring, inspirational stuff, from Churchill.

Zelensky offered a riff, unmistakable, even imitative, in its Churchillian resonance, in address to the British House of Commons.

"We will fight till the end, at sea, in the air," the T-shirted Zelensky promised, his tone impassioned, his audience rapt, ready to break into applause. All the applause culminating in a standing ovation. Zelensky's voice, of course, no match for that of one roughly sand-papered by decades of chomping on a cigar and marinated to ton-al perfection by a steady diet of whiskey and soda (never neat, was Churchill's habit), champagne and wine (at lunch and dinner, re-spectively).

No matter. It was the Churchillian spirit that Zelensky imbibed. And imbibe it he did splendidly. Modulated by direct address. Be-fitting a man dedicated to a military chic entirely of his own making (with a nod to Ché, admittedly, as to designers high and low, all of whom appear to be unable to break out of the cycle that is producing the latest camo, in high, middlebrow, or lowbrow/"street" fashion) Zelensky exuded a kind of reluctant bullishness. Churchillian in con-struction, of course: "We will fight in the forests, in the fields, on the shores, on the streets." Equal parts rural guerilla and last-ditch urban defender of the nation. In Zelensky's promise, that was, of course, also an appeal, directly to his friend "Boris" (when the nation is at stake, sartorial rules and parliamentary regulations must be dispensed with; everything but the struggle to survive is decoration), was the antic-ipation of hand-to-hand combat: Ukrainians, soldiers and civilians, insofar as the distinction continued to obtain, doing direct battle with their Russian invaders. Rousseau, in a sense, Ukrainians with ev-erything to lose, beginning with the prospect of being held in chains by Russia, should they fail to defend their nation.

WHAT WE HAVE IN COMMON

Imitation, then, as the sincerest form of political flattery. Imitation is how, à la Dale Carnegie, you win friends and influence people. Those whom you hope to recruit to your side in the hour of your deepest national need. Imitation, however, also as the only way to effectively communicate the desperation of your situation. Imitation as the appeal to your audience to not only walk in your shoes but to remember how they themselves walked in shoes that matched yours, almost exactly. Only before you did. History, as the bringing to life of the struggle that your audience endured before you did.

Always knowing how to hit the right note.

In his address to the Israeli Knesset, Zelensky relied upon a more geographical sense of history, reminding his audience that Golda Meir had been born in Kyiv. Again, the invocation of Meir's birthplace, before she ascended to the highest office in Israel, is meant to demonstrate a bond between two nations—the leader of one nation traces her roots to another place, a place now under siege. In appealing to a shared history, the ties that bind impose, no matter how it is received, responsibility upon the audience. It is, in the case of Meir being mobilized, a blood tie. A sacred one, we might say. How does one refuse the sanctity of the ties that bind? How does one turn one's back on history? On, in this case, Israel's own history? To deny that bond is akin to choosing Abramovich over a founding member of the Israeli state, a former Minister of Labor and Minister of Foreign Affairs (secretary of state), and, of course, Israel's first, and only, to date, female Prime Minister. The oligarch over the Israeli "Iron Lady," Zionist veteran of the kibbutz;[83] the Ukrainian diasporized from Kyiv to Wisconsin to Israel.

However, just because you hit the right note doesn't mean that you'll get the response you desire. Instead, even after Zelensky's address, Israel refused to sell its Pegasus spyware to Ukraine (and Estonia) because "Israel feared that selling the cyberweapon to adversaries of Russia would damage Israel's relationship with the Kremlin."[84]

Key to the work of Carl Schmitt, a German philosopher sympathetic to the Nazis, is the distinction between "friend and enemy." There are moments, such as the request to Israel to acquire Pegasus, Zelensky might be forgiven for being unable to uphold that distinction. How does the "hurt" that Israel suggests it might incur (as in the case of Abramovich) and the prospect of "damaged" relationship to Moscow equate to on-going Ukrainian death?

Golda Meir's birthplace can be invoked, but it is an invocation that, when push comes to shove, can be ignored. Sometimes, much as you hit the right rhetorical note, it will do you no good at all. Your audience can hear your appeal, they understand its logic, they might even admire your reaching out to them specifically, but they are more than happy to turn a deaf ear to it. Or, should I say, a dead ear. Better still, an ear deaf to the death of your people.

Still, hitting the right note matters.

By making clear to your audience, the House of Commons, through a language that they have long taken to be theirs but which you are now laying claim to, how their language belongs to a history that you now share, by dint of bitter experience, unwanted, unavoidable, imposed upon you by a risible foreign force, that history has joined you, one people to another. You are now bound together, a tie has been forged. You share a language: the language of the struggle to survive. All House of Commons' Churchillian poetry, rousing as it is, is now claimed, strategically, by Zelensky. You bring their poetry alive to them. You speak their poetry, poetically, as though it were nothing more than political commonsense. You agree on this: there is fighting to be done today as there was a fight to be engaged those many decades ago. And, in the process of all this sharing, a responsibility is now imposed upon your audience. You remind them of the responsibility they expected of themselves. A responsibility not only to themselves, but to everyone in the non- or anti-Axis world. Such a world as Churchill named, which included British colonies, unironically. The "democratic world." (But democracy would follow, soon enough, in the colonies, beginning in India a scant two years after the end of WWII.) That world appealed to, that world which would invoke those self-same rights to self-determination, democracy and freedom from colonialism which would follow when fascism was defeated. No one needs reminding, even as I've just done so, that to be found in Churchill's stirring speech was the seed of the Empire's demise.

In his speech to the House of Commons, Zelensky sought to put paid to the possible germination of that imperial seed, no matter that it is but a withered, beaten husk. Brutal, *Russky Mir*, like all imperialisms. To make Bob Marley's declamation of "Sheriff John Brown" ("Always hated me") unrecognizable to the reggae star, "Kill it before it grows." The metaphor that is here attributed to Zelensky is unfortunate in its violence. It is, nonetheless, a warning that is no longer prescient. All claims to prescience can be said to have died in 2008 with Russia's invasion of Crimea. But the warning remains urgent. Maybe more so now than ever. That seed should have been killed in 2008. Look what it hath wrought.

At the time of writing.

In his address to the British House of Commons, Zelensky made Ukraine heirs to the best British political tradition. In so doing, he made the British responsible to their own history. He made them responsible, regardless of whether members of the House of Commons chose to acknowledge it, for Ukraine's struggle against Putin. "Boris" was put in the position, whether or not he found it uncomfortable was not a question to be indulged, of having to choose. To choose: between good or evil, as Zelensky put it in his address to the Israeli Knesset. Good and evil, not terms that Churchill invoked, but apropos for Zelensky's moment, for his method. To choose between Zelensky and Putin. A pity that Zelensky did not invoke Navalny.

In a strange way, in presenting Boris Johnson with that choice, Zelensky reminded his audience, Johnson, personally, but also the House of Commons and the British people more generally, of what as at stake. "Boris," the Prime Minister's first name, invoked as a form of familiarity but also a metonym: the part standing in for the whole; "Boris" standing as representative of the entire United Kingdom. "Boris" as both a marker of personal intimacy—two leaders who know each other—but also as the name used to name every other subject of Her Majesty's kingdom. A personal address, then, encapsulated in the name "Boris." Zelensky speaking through "Boris" to each and every Briton. Lifting them all out of themselves.

Hardly a run-of-the-mill English name, "Boris." So perhaps history intended Johnson, an ordinary British name, to be the Prime Minister in the time that would offer up a Slavic address. In Slavic "Borislava," designates, "bori," "battle," and "slava," "fame" or "glory." In calling upon "Boris" to do what Ukraine needed, the British Prime Minister was being asked to join the "battle" for "fame" and "glory," a "battle" that had already secured Zelensky "fame" and "glory." "Boris" was now being asked to sup at the same historical table. First, however, "Boris" would have to pay the price of admission. British support. British support so that Zelensky, as he promised to the Ukrainian people and the House of Commons, would, in Churchill's spirit, never have to surrender. He would fight. On sea, on land, in the air, in the forests. By way of a spectacular exit, Zelensky taunted Putin: "I'm not hiding. I'm not afraid of anyone."[85]

In truth, fear, retreat, compromise or seeking refuge in a safe location are all denied to Zelensky. He has, like Churchill, no alternative. He must stand and fight. That decision was made when Zelensky issued his first commonsense statement. "I don't need a ride." Nothing less, that statement, than a declaration of intent.

When Zelensky played a history teacher conscripted into saving his country, he could not have imagined that would literally have to declare himself, before the world, time and again, the "Servant of the People." The "Servant of the People" desperately in need of "ammo." "Please, sir, can I have some (more)?" Zelensky cast as the latter-day Oliver Twist, assuming an incarnation of which Dickens would most certainly have approved, no matter that the militarization of that alimentary question would be most unfamiliar to that great chronicler of the ills of nineteenth-century British industrial society.

WHAT I NEED FROM MY FRIENDS

"I call on you to do more."

Zelensky, Address to the Joint Houses of Congress, March 16th, 2022.

If there one thing that has become apparent with every Zelensky address to the various parliaments that have granted him an audience, it is this. Zelensky is masterfully adept at tailoring his message to his audience. He knows his audience. He knows what rhetorical buttons to push. Churchill in Britain's darkest hour for the House of Commons, the specter of a divided Europe when he spoke before the German Bundestag. South Korean reminded of its battle for existence. Zelensky tells his audience almost exactly what they expect to hear, but, still, he surprises them. In spite of themselves. His audience is never prepared for precisely what it is they prepared themselves for.

As one might have expected, then, in his address to the joint Houses of Congress, Zelensky drew on Martin Luther King, Jr. This is the form, a form made distinctive and substantive, that Zelensky gave to King's "I have a dream:" "Is this a lot to ask for, to create a no-fly zone over Ukraine to save people? Is this too much to ask, humanitarian no-fly zone, something that Russia would not be able to terrorize our free cities?"[86] Zelensky, dreaming of a "no-fly zone?" What could be more practical? What could save more Ukrainian lives? Zelensky, dreaming of a Ukrainian sky free of Russian menace. And death, the death that relentless bombing of Ukrainian cities from Dnipro in the east to Mariupol in the south to Lviv in the west. Lviv, just 100 kilometers from the Polish border, where NATO currently begins, and with it, fleeing Ukrainians believe, safety from Russian aggression does too. For how long?

King's dream has never sounded so strategic. Ensuring, protecting, Ukrainian life, that is, if not the mountain top, then certainly the foothills of a free Ukrainian plateau that Zelensky would like to secure. A sky free of menace, and then Zelensky can begin to dream of being free, free at last.

This is what political allies who find themselves under siege do. They ask their allies, historic or newly minted, for help. "Please, sir." "Please." But, asking. Imploring. Not begging. Appealing to everyone's better instincts. Or, angels, even. Lincolnesque. But speaking not at the beginning of the end of a battle, but, speaking as though he does not know, cannot know, for how long the Ukrainian people will have struggle. And no guarantee that they will endure.

Appealing through a rhetorical strategy entirely predictable, all the expected evocations, all the names and events each of his audience hold dearest—Normandy, Pearl Harbor, a divided Berlin. Telling everyone what they wanted to hear and lifting them up, lifting them out of themselves, in his telling them. Servant, yes, and master too. Master of making of the request, again, a responsibility to which his audience must answer. Making them accountable to their better, if not their best, selves.

And practical, insistently so, to a fault:

> I am grateful to you for the resolution which recognizes all those who commit crimes against Ukraine, against the Ukrainian people, as war criminals. However, now it is true in the darkest time for our country, for the whole of Europe, I call on you to do more. New packages of sanctions are needed constantly, every week, until the Russian military machine stops. Restrictions are needed for everyone on whom this unjust regime is based. (Ibid)

Churchill's "darkest hour" extended, "darkest time." This time that must be brought to an end. Those who have the power and the military means to bring this horrific time to a close must do so. Forthwith. 1%. Those who have the power and the military might now find themselves presented with a searing question: do they have the political will? An anti-Gramscian Gramsci. Be done, for now, with Gramsci's "pessimism of the intellect, optimism of the will." In its place, optimism through the intellect, the will to remain true to optimism. To phrase the matter another way, is political will solely the province of those who dream? "I call on you to do more." Willing his audience to venture into parts of their national selves of which they are afraid? The specter of a war, a nuclear war, a biological war, a chemical war, that Putin holds as his trump card if NATO as a collectivity or the U.S. takes as its responsibility the imposition of a no-fly zone over Ukraine?

An awesome quandary presented to Prime Minister Johnson, Chancellor Olaf Scholtz, and President Biden. How many lives must be given up in the name of the very real prospect that is global nuclear disaster?

VOLODYMYR ZELENSKY, THE ST. CHRISTOPHER OF DEMOCRACY

No matter. It is not a question that will dissipate. It hangs about, threateningly, as self-indictment and self-preservation do unholy battle within all national selves. What risks are to be taken? How can long can the decision be postponed? If the prospect of Armageddon is a real one, so is the very real specter that will be the future haunting that will go by the name "Ukraine, 2022." February 24th, 2022. A date made auspicious and deadly by Putin. February 24th, as Zelensky reminded the world, is an inauspicious date in history. On February 24th, 1920, the Nazi party was founded in Germany. Already inscribed in, and by, the date of Putin's invasion was a historic warning. Shakespearean, were Julius Caesar's "Ides of March" reinscribed as the "Fate of February."

Those who refuse to learn from history, as Marx warned us, are doomed to repeat it.

The "Servant of the People" come as a messenger from the past to caution the world against the horrors that the future holds. Less "Servant of the People," then, and more Shakespearean soothsayer. Less a Falstaff and more a Caliban from eastern Europe. A Caliban who wants no part of the invaders from Russia.

A glorious role, then, for Zelensky. Promoted, through the responsibility that he imposes without apology, "I need," from "Servant of the People" to under siege spokesperson for . . . For democracy, dare one say? All his addresses, as much to the political gatherings and the politicians gathered there as to all the nation's peoples who are represented in these democratic bodies, to those peoples who understand themselves to live in democratic societies.

#ArmUkraineNow.

As Russia intensified its onslaught on eastern Ukraine, the US and EU nations such as Germany and Poland appear, *at the time of writing*, to be, in some measure or other (hardly sufficient, but, ...) responding to that call.[87]

Volodymyr Zelensky: the St. Christopher of democracy.

How will he bear this undue burden?

Will anyone relieve him of this burden?

Will anyone share it with him? Biden, Johnson, Bennett, Scholtz?

"Mirror, mirror, on the wall, who is the most democratic of us all?"

Who cannot look into the mirror of democracy? Cannot look there for fearing of encountering tens of thousands of Ukrainian dead? Soldiers, civilians, men, women, children, even a Holocaust survivor? Who will write this history, using as their writing "instrument," as the Jewish Algerian philosopher Jacques Derrida would have it, only the bare hand that holds within it "cinders and ashes?" That is the only material with which to write the Shoah. What a terrible specter is already discernible now. Clearly outlined, already haunting us.

"A specter is haunting Europe." And the world too.

A specter that long ago began to make itself immanent. Georgia, Ukraine, now, again, Ukraine. No longer a specter, then, but an actor fully formed.

That actor who is either historically ignorant or, worse, possesses a sharp sense of the dates most infamous, and therefore memorable, in the history of terror.

An actor, we should remember, long since enabled by the likes of Angela Merkel, the former German Chancellor who was the very instantiation of *realpolitik*. Long feted as a stabilizing influence in Europe, praised for her leadership in the EU, what the current crisis in Ukraine reveals is the cost of Merkel's proximity to Putin.[88] A fluent Russian speaker she was, Merkel, Chancellor from 2005 until she stepped down in 2021; Merkel's tenure saw increasingly friendly relations between Germany (and the EU) and Russia. During Merkel's last term in office, Germany increased its dependence on Russian oil and gas, and Merkel treated Putin as though he were a good faith actor. Even in the wake of Crimea, Merkel urged caution, preached the virtues of diplomacy, and, as a consequence, between her and Obama, pretty much gave Putin a free ride on his illegal annexation.

Commonsense, of course, teaches us that if you concede an inch, it won't be long before you've given up a whole yard.

Bismarckian *realpolitik* is not only a study in political pragmatism. It is also an object lesson in acting on the inviolable principle of self-interest. A sort of Hippocratic oath for politicians, inflected with cynicism, of course. Politician, do your self-interest no harm. If Germany could secure oil and gas from Russia at the most economic rates, if Russia did not (directly) threaten Germany and Europe, then all manner of aggressions could be tolerated. Overlooked, if necessary.

Under Merkel, Germany's military readiness declined. Not in itself a bad thing, of course, but it has left her successor Scholtz with the unenviable task of getting the country's military up to speed while facing an existential threat.

It would, of course, be inaccurate to suggest that Putin "played" Merkel. Germany's first female leader, and one who emerged out of the old East Germany, showed herself way too canny a political operator for that.

However, Merkel, as *de facto* EU leader, failed to take seriously the threat(s) that Russia could pose. She was not sufficiently alert to the logic and historical imperative that is *Russky Mir*. The Russian imperial dream, as history has taught us (a truth that obtains as much in Czarist Russia as it did in the USSR), is a stubborn political animal. The blood of *Russky Mir* flows as much in Czarists as it does in Communists, post-Communists, and good old-fashioned imperial capitalists. Experts at state capture too. Putin, it goes without saying, ticks all those boxes.

Because Merkel dropped her guard, played footsie with Putin, in Russian, of course, the EU did too. A costly game, this, follow-the-leader.

Merkel, complicit? Not exactly. But the former Chancellor is by no means blameless. As that Prussian master political strategist,

Count Otto von Bismarck knew all too well, realpolitik is only an effective practice when infused with a healthy dose of suspicion.

Be careful not only of how you do business, but who you do business with. Merkel forgot, or, as bad, ignored Bismarck's teachings.

Appeasement, as Neville Chamberlain quickly learned, never ends well.

Again, as history warned Merkel (who seemed to have forgotten all about Chamberlain's ill-fated compromise that was not a compromise), appeasement does not only have one dramatic form. The leader descending from a plane, waving a piece of paper guaranteeing peace. That is simply the most dramatic form of appeasement. It can as easily find its first expression in a blind eye being turned here, making an undeserved accommodation for a political ally there. Appeasement doesn't always begin in Munich. It doesn't happen all at once. It can be a patient and incipient creature.

At the very least, one would have hoped that the event of the Sudetenland would have cast an ominous shadow on Russia's invasion of Crimea. At the very least, one would have hoped that Merkel would, in light of Russia's war and the Bucha atrocities, have taken the opportunity to revise her position. Not so. Merkel remains wedded to her position that the EU was correct in its decision to refuse Ukraine admission to the organization.[89] EU membership would, of course, have bound all the EU members states to come Ukraine's defense. "An injury to one." It might have given Putin cause for pause. Had Ukraine been admitted, Putin would have faced the military might of all (EU member nations).

BENEDICT OF NURSIA

In his address to the House of Commons, Zelensky also achieved a political reintegration that seemed, before *that* date, February 24th, 2022, impossible. Ironically, it is Putin who has brought *that* date back into history. By choosing to invade on *that* day (why not a day earlier or a day later? A week later? We know that he did not want to rain—reign?—on the parade that was Xi's Winter Olympics, but its not as though a slight bringing forward of the date of invasion or delay would have made that much of a difference, would it?), Putin's historical ignorance, arrogance or complete disregard for history ensured that he will now have added Russian ignominy to Nazi infamy. Turns out Ukrainian history teachers read history. Even those who only play a history teacher take the time to read history.

For a political leader so intent on his own singularity, the Czarist president determined to be defined by his apartness (that is, his *Russky Mir* exceptionality), there are few worse dates he could have chosen. Appropriate that he blundered so historically, one could argue, because the short, triumphal campaign he imagined, being welcomed in Kyiv as the grand liberator, has turned—*at the time of writing*—into a more than two month-long military slog.

A slog in which, despite superior Russian firepower, Ukrainians have mounted a stout defense. Even when Russian troops advance, they have often found themselves unable to hold their ground. Indeed, around the major cities especially, whatever gains Putin's forces have made, they find themselves driven once more into retreat by inspired Ukrainian determination to retake their cities. Not quite the catastrophe that was Napoleon's Western Front, but, so far, a failure of colossal proportions. February 24th, 2022: this is when the end began for Czar Bloodymir.

In his address to the House of Commons, in his being welcomed, applauded, lauded, one is also tempted to say "lorded," made "Lord Zelensky, Defender of European Democracy," Zelensky (momentarily) cast aside the whole matter of Brexit. Zelensky was not only speaking to the British House of Commons, to his friend Boris, to the British people, he was speaking to all within that extended audience, to Britons the length and breadth of their sacred isle, to the millions watching in Europe and across the world. Specifically, he was speaking to everyone as Europeans.

In a Europe fractured along ideological lines, divided between the democracies and the dictators, an EU trying, with only moderate success, to bring those dictators (Orban and his ilk; a dictatorial, ethno-nationalist impulse with significant purchase in Italy, always on the horizon in France as Marie le Pen once more battles Macron for the presidency, unapologetic in Poland, and so on), Russia's attack on Ukraine created the opportunity for something on the order of a "European" identity, a continent with a reinvigorated sense of self and historical purpose, to come into being. This creation, or, recreation, of course, runs entirely contrary to Putin's plan to stay Europe: to keep it, whether in the guise of NATO or the EU, as far from Russia's borders as possible; and, to fuel, in whatever way he could, dissension with European ranks. A Europe dependent on Russia for its energy supplies (oil and natural gas), a Europe made increasingly, so it would seem, insignificant on the global stage, a stage now dominated by the U.S., China, and with India, at least India before the Covid-crisis, apparently on the rise. Putin created the opportunity for Zelensky to return Europe, much to its own surprise, to relevance again. And, not just relevant in an ancillary way, that is, the extension of U.S. military power in Europe (NATO), but as a *polis*—a political community—charged, by history, with an Idea.

What is more, Zelensky is addressing less the politically elected leaders of Europe than he is proposing the Idea of Europe to *all* the people of Europe. Proposing the Idea.

An old-fashioned, Kantian, claim, perhaps, that the Idea could not only return to Europe, from whence it came—the Idea of Europe, but that the Idea could also animate a mode of being in the world, in relation to its neighbors. That the Idea could provide the groundwork for a rethinking of relations amongst the various national units that constitute Europe. A foundation that might lead to self-examination of the philosophical project that is "Europe." That is "democracy." The Idea returning to Europe, the Idea returning Europe to itself, in a much altered but not unrecognizable way. That is, a Europe seeking to find its place in the world having undergone decolonization and knowing itself as being imperfect—politically, culturally, in terms of race, immigration, the anti-LGBTQ+ hostility in some quarters, and so on—in its collectivity. Europe as undoubtedly imperfect in its constituent units, for the reasons just cited. Having faced several economic crises (Greece in 2015 perhaps most notably), having weathered a range of conflicts, addressed as "Europe" by Zelensky Europe is now compelled, by its own history as much as anything else, to present itself as a bulwark against fascist militarism. An imperfect, bureaucratic, parliamentary democracy, but it must now face Zelensky as he addresses Europe.

Frequently at odds with itself. The Idea of Europe, maybe not fully aligned with the representation offered above, is now charged with the responsibility of taking its place in a world under threat. A Europe forced, despite itself, to its easternmost outpost, Poland. East of Poland, how far does Europe now understand itself to extend? Finland, Sweden, deciding that the time is now. New geo-political parameters, bringing with it at least two new questions. Where does Europe begin? Where does Europe end? What is Europe's Idea of Europe? In the shadow of these inquiries, the more pressing question lurks, ominously: can Europe rise to that which it is being asked to be? *Carpe diem*, the moment for taking up that difficulty, for engaging in that careful and surely painful self-confrontation, is now. The hour is upon Europe.

Can Europe answer Zelensky's call, a call already affirmatively responded to on March 24th, 2022, when thousands of people the world over,[90] from Colombia to the U.S. to various parts of Asia and Africa, making their opposition to Putin known? Salient, however, was the massive protest that took place in front of the EU buildings in Brussels, where the EU is headquartered. All those Ukrainian flags being boisterously waved told its own story.

Because of Zelensky's direct address to it, Europe must now inquire into its own self-presentation. It must decide how to both encapsulate what is "best and brightest" about it and decide what is in most urgent need of renovation. Europe, thrust, again, into history, this time in a manner hardly of its own making.

Zelensky implicitly presenting Europe to itself as that mode of political being that he imagines, understands, and, most important, wants Europe to be. Zelensky turning to Europe in the hour of his most desperate need, the effect of which might be, as has been suggested, returning Europe to an Idea-lized incarnation of itself.

The "Idea," as offered here, derives from the German philosopher Immanuel Kant's concept of "transcendental idealism." For Kant there is a distinction between what we can experience, that which we know in the world, and that which we cannot. What we cannot Kant names "supersensible," the most notable of which is "God" and the "soul." Kant stakes a great deal on the superiority of experience. Kant, we can say, as a scientific philosopher—a thinker who assigned precedence to that which was observable. That for which there was proof.

For our purposes, however, we do not adhere (too) strictly to Kant's distinction. Experience and the "supersensible," we are proposing, cannot be kept apart quite so rigorously. While we acknowledge that experience takes precedence over "God," contained within Kant's "supersensible" is a recognition of something beyond, something that exceeds experience, something for which human beings yearn. Hence, "God," hence our ascription to the metaphysical concept of the "soul." That is, an essence deeper, more profound, than that which our everyday experience can access. However, it must be said that whatever notion of the "supersensible" we subscribe to— or reject, as the case might be—it is only out of our experience, our thinking of experience, that we can gain entry to, are able to construct an idea of, the "supersensible."

Let us agree, commonsensically and provisionally, to define human inclining toward the "supersensible" as a reaching for our better, if not quite our best, selves. Better selves we are inspired to become. Better selves for which we reach with a special commitment and intensity in moments of historical—or personal—crisis. Appeals to which we moved to respond. Compelled by our better selves. Lincoln's "Gettysburg Address," JFK's "Ask not what your country can do for you" speech, the example of Gandhi's self-imposed fasting to secure independence for India, Malala risking her life to ensure the right to education for girls in Pakistan.

Out of Zelensky's words and actions, his experience, and the "supersensible" impulse it evokes in the world, his appeals to us to answer to a higher calling, emerges the Idea of a re-created Europe. Zelensky is appealing not only to all Europeans' better selves. He is implicitly asking all Europeans to embrace the possibility of a Europe remade. A Europe remade in the geo-political image implicit in his call to Europe. A Europe that now begins, and ends, in Crimea. A Europe in which all bear responsibility for all. A Europe that now must live up to the Idea of a humanity equal in all respects. In word and deed. "An injury to one ..."

A Europe which, in demonstrating its willingness to take to its bosom Ukrainian refugees must now show that self-same propensity for unquestioned hospitality to those fleeing similar atrocities, atrocities taking place far beyond its borders—Africa, Afghanistan, Latin America, Asia—that has produced a similar exodus of people trying to escape violence. A Europe that will not, even as Bulgaria commendably took in a large number of Ukrainian refugees, tolerate the Bulgarian Prime Minister Kiril Petkov's lamentable racism: "These people are Europeans. These people are intelligent, they are educated people. ... This is not the refugee wave we have been used to ..."[91] The question of race, one which Europe has long struggled with, must now be reconsidered, if only in relation to the plight of refugees—the race of the refugees, the face of the refugees, the racism directed at those refugees who are not white, like the Ukrainians. That is, Europe's response to the Ukrainian refugee crisis—*at the time of writing* almost 11 million refugees, with some 6 million still trapped in Ukraine—must become the only acceptable standard for how to deal with refugees. From Poland, on its doorstep, to

Ireland, faraway in the North Atlantic, Ukrainians are offered refuge. To make of the (French—*refugié,*—a word that emerged in the late-17th century) root of the word "refugee"—"one who flees to a refuge or shelter or place of safety; one who in times of persecution or political disorder flees to a foreign country for safety"[92]—an enduring plan for political action.

A Europe, in short, that will not tolerate ethno-nationalism in any guise. A Europe that keeps a keen eye on the likes of Viktor Orban, Nigel Farage, Matteo Salvini, and anyone with the last name Le Pen. Vigilance as the watchword for the Zelensky-inspired Idea of Europe.

A Europe that shows itself willing to risk life and limb in the cause of a universally equal humanity. Determined to remain steadfast in the face of any unprovoked, unjust attack on human beings, a Europe that will defend any and all of its constituents; a Europe that will repel an attack on any of its constituent parts. That is the Idea that Zelensky does not so much incarnate, though that it is a sustainable claim, but the Idea which he has reactivated, and in doing so has put into global circulation. The Idea made, if not "supersensible," then maybe indispensable for the world which we must make. Must make so as to put an end to Putin and his kind.

In the germ of the Kantian Idea, then, there always lurks a not-so submerged utopian impulse. (If Kant would not have his Idea "transcend" into the unscientific "supersensible," then what he offers is at least a way of bridging, of bringing together, the experiential and the "supersensible." Body and soul, if you prefer, edging nearer to each other.) The impulse that urges Europe to be its best Enlightenment self. That self of the late-eighteenth century to which French Revolutionaries first gave philosophical voice, first gave democratic shape and political form to. A voice that cried out against monarchical tyranny and exploitation. A voice that found democratic fulfillment in Toussaint L'Ouverture. A democratic shape founded upon the destruction of an oppressive class system, a project that remains, universally, to be completed. A political form that still rests upon the universal franchise and the right of the people to determine their own future.

A project far removed from that of Benedict of Nursia. It might be, however, that every age in Europe demands its own Benedict, a Nursian visionary suited to its own needs. If not a visionary, then, perhaps, at least, a European optimist who retains more than a smidgeon of Gramscian pessimism. Just to keep us honest. Willing Europe to be what Ukraine needs it to be. Lifting Europe, as it were, out of itself. Making it rise above itself.

Benedict of Nursia returned as Jewish Zelensky, Patron Saint of Europe.

EUROPEANS RATHER THAN INDIVIDUAL SOVEREIGNTIES

In order to bring this Idea into being, in his addressing not only European political leaders, Zelensky has taken to addressing Europeans *as* Europeans. That is, even when he is addressing individual legislatures, be that British or Italian, Zelensky is also speaking to their constituents. Speaking to them not only as citizens (again, as Italian or British) but as national citizens invited to understand themselves as political subjects who can now, in the wake of and because of Putin's war, stake a claim to a larger constituency. That is, Zelensky's address suggests that the European Union, as it is currently constituted, is all good and well for facilitating trade and the unfettered—no borders, the SCHENGEN zone and all that—movement of people, but it has failed in a crucial aspect.

The European Union has failed to make Europeans out of its constituent member states. National identities prevail because that is how the Spanish or the Dutch understand themselves within the EU. Because that is how they present themselves to the other member nations in the EU.

It may be that it is only in a crisis, especially in a crisis that erupts out of war, that an other, a completely different, sense of self might be thought into being. A sense of self grown historically impatient with the provincialization of identity under the guise of pan-Europeanization. That is, the EU pretends to, aspires to, a sense of commonality, a shared sense of political, economic, and cultural self, but that is neither extant not what Zelensky hopes to extract from his audience.

What Zelensky may be seeking is something on a higher order. It may very well begin with the recognition that to be Italian or Greek in the EU is to be, well, Italian or Greek. It may prove impossible to dislodge so deeply ingrained—in history, culture, political memory—a sense of the self that is grounded in the nation. Europeanness, such as it exists, is a prosthetic, an appendage, a name, a flag, that can be called into service whenever it is convenient. Europeanness can be tacked on, displayed on a T-shirt at a political rally denouncing Putin. It lacks, this secondary Europeanness, something less tangible, but is nevertheless vital to the Europeanness that Zelensky is trying to call into being.

Europeanness as prosthetic lacks spirit. Spirit, *Geist*, a concept given to us by G.W.F. Hegel, the thinker who succeeded Kant as the most important German philosopher of his day. *Geist* is what is needed. As we know, Kant is renowned for privileging experience over the "supersensible." In terms of what Zelensky's mode of address seems to call for, however, it might be possible to reinforce our earlier proposal that we think experience and the "supersensible" together. That is, it is to a European *Geist*, in which might legitimately be detected a ghostliness, to which Zelensky is appealing.

Zelensky calls on the *Geist* first because it is out of (a) spirit rather than experience that Europeanness can be born. Experience is what is known. Experience tells us, reminds us, of what we know. Because of that which is familiar, it is the familiar to which we, out of habit, turn and which we expect to sustain us. *Geist*, however, is something else. It is a call from the unknown, or, at best, from that which is only barely known. *Geist* is an appeal that issues from beyond our experience. The power of *Geist* resides in its unfamiliarity. *Geist* unsettles us, causes us to doubt how it is we are in the world, and why it is we are the way we are in the world. *Geist* is the most direct confrontation with our deepest fears about ourselves, and, as such, it throws everything that we presume about ourselves, all our actions, from the mundane that is our humdrum lives to our most hallowed practices, all that is we understand ourselves to know, into question.

Zelensky's *Geist* asks us to consider the effects of ethno-nationalism, to think, as if for the first time, our investment in it. It asks that we interrogate our attachments to language, culture, and, yes, blood. As such, Zelensky's *Geist* is a potentially divisive force. The *Geist* marks, at this moment in Europe's history, an unmistakable fault line. A fault line that will enforce a division between those we are irredeemably wedded to ethno-nationalism and those in search of another way of being in Europe. Those who, like Zelensky, but under markedly different material conditions, yearn for something else. Even if that something else remains poorly defined, an indiscernible *Geist*, but so hauntingly, tantalizingly present, nonetheless. A *Geist* so full of promise, offering a prospect as yet unknown to experience. *Geist* as that "supersensible" force that allows a Zelensky-inspired madness to emerge into, and as, its own method.

And yet, *Geist* is not entirely unknown. It is already known to us as the bringing to life once more the spirit of "An injury to one is an injury to all." It remains only for us, now attentive to the *Geist* that Zelensky has stirred into life, to reanimate that commitment. It might just be the speaking of Zelensky's *Geist*, the spirit in which he issues his plea to us to begin the project that is, not to put too fine a Kantian point on it, the Idea of Europe.

The *Geist* poses a forceful a question because what it asks can only be answered either negatively or affirmatively. Will Europe continue to trust to its experience, or will it give itself up in the cause of *Geist*? Lurking in that question is already the makings of an indictment. Is Europe really satisfied with its experience as it stands? Is another way not possible? Must it always be thus? Confronted with this threat or the other?

It may, of course, be possible to see in the challenges that *Geist* presents the opening up of an entirely new, more livable, non-violent, equitable, set of experiences. The Zelenskian project as the desire for producing a way of being European vigorously at odds with all ethno-nationalist practices. *Geist* as neither soul nor God but as a template for a different, distinctly European experience. *Geist* as that intuited mode of being European that is nothing more than answering the call emanating from within the rubble of Mariupol and Kyiv, a call that cannot be drowned out by Russian bombs, a call that seeks to silence *Russky Mir* and all other such unsuppressed imperial ambitions.

A call that Benedict of Nursia, in his best incarnation, might not only have answered but could very well, had he imagined such a political prospect, have issued himself.

That task, instead, has fallen to Volodymyr Zelensky.

METHOD IN THE MADNESS

In non-regulation fatigues, Zelensky has risen to the occasion of Europe that is not-yet but could, because of the call that Zelensky has issued, very well already be emerging. In all probability only in outline, but still ...

Nevertheless, the call is audible, if only barely. The project is being sketched with every act of Ukrainian resistance, with every Ukrainian military success, big or small,[93] with every address that Zelensky undertakes. With every morning update that Governor Kim issues.

In so doing, it might be more apt now to speak of a newly minted patron saint for Europe.

It may very well turn out that there is more method than madness to Zelensky than anyone, Zelensky himself included, could have anticipated on February 25th, 2022.

What seemed like madness, "I don't need a ride," marks the very moment that the Zelensky method came into being. "I don't need a ride" is the precise moment that the madness showed its method.

NOTES

1 140 Companies That Have Pulled Out of Russia | Kiplinger; Why over 450 companies have withdrawn from Russia, and why some haven't - Marketplace

2 Ibid.

3 The Palestine story on JSTOR

4 The companies that are not boycotting Russia (nypost.com)

5 Here's where Russian oligarchs and their families own property in NYC (nypost.com)

6 Beverly Gage, "The Accidental President," *The New Yorker*, March 14, 2022, 70.

7 Fintan O'Toole: Russia's 'feral' capitalism is a threat to democracy | Watch (msn.com)

8 https://www.msn.com/en-us/news/world/burkina-faso-tribu nal-sentences-ex-leader-compaore-to-life/ar-AAVVhn6?oc id=entnewsntp&cvid=88febc8da7f2496bbe2a42dd1a43e61d

9 A secessionist movement designed to undo the project that Lumumba intended to set in motion, a movement that, while the Belgians may have been the prime instigators (and canny in their turn to Tshombe, the key political figure in a province considered economically vital by Europe and the U.S.), neither the U.S. nor the United Nations, which was supposed to secure peace, are, to say the least, blameless.

10 Already Finland, which shares an 830 mile (1,340 kilometer) border with Russia, and Sweden, after remaining steadfastly outside of the North Atlantic Treaty Organization (NATO, which came into being on Truman's watch), now appear ready to apply for fast-tracked membership. With the US's backing. And angering Putin, who thunders on about possible military retaliation. See Putin's bullying backfires as Finland and Sweden edge closer to joining NATO - CNN

11 Ukraine President Volodomyr Zelenskyy addressed South Korea's

Parliament : NPR

12 See Mujib Mashal, "What's India's Stance? To Take No Stance," *The New York Times* Thursday, March 31, 2022.

13 See, for example, Andrew E. Kramer, "In Retaliating, Ukraine Sends Signal to the World," *The New York Times*, Friday, March 25, 2022. And Julian E. Barnes, "Why the U.S. Misjudged Ukrainians' Will to Fight, and Why It Matters" (Ibid).

14 See, Valerie Hopkins, "Exiles of Belarus Join the Battle to Fight for Ukraine's Cause, and Their Own," *The New York Times*, Friday, March 25, 2022. Hopkins notes that the Belarussians have formed a unit, the "Kastus Kalinouski battalion," to fight the Russians. Kalinouski, it is worth noting, was a "19th-century Belarussian who led an uprising against the Russian Empire, on March 9."

15 Jair Bolsonaro, Brazil's president has insisted on his nation's neutrality. See "Bolsonaro finally reveals where Brazil will stand regarding Ukraine — MercoPress See "Brazil Won't Take Sides Over Russia's Invasion of Ukraine - Foreign Minister" | World News | US News

16 "Ukraine: Why India is not criticising Russia over invasion - BBC News" and India's position on Russia-Ukraine conflict steadfast and consistent: President Kovind (republicworld.com)

17 Chinese artist unveils painting for Ukraine, 'which has already won' (msn.com)

18 Thomas Gibbons-Neff, Michael Schwirtz and Eric Schmitt, "Russia Strikes Hard as It Pushes to Seize Donbas Region, *The New York Times,* Wednesday, April 20, 2022.

19 Stone has since denounced Putin over the Ukraine invasion. See, among others, Oliver Stone condemns Putin's 'aggression in Ukraine', says 'Russia was wrong to invade' (republicworld.com); "If Oliver Stone didn't regret his Putin interviews before – he will now" (telegraph.co.uk) What can also be gleaned from the "Putin Interviews" are some of the reasons for the Russian public's support of Putin. These include returning the country to a level of functionality and efficiency in the wake of Boris Yeltsin's disastrous reign; restoring Russia's place in the global order as a major

international force, a position severely affected after the fall of the Soviet Union; improving a much degraded Russian military; and, not least, improving the daily quality of life for a large section of the Russian population.

20 As we know, the newly re-elected Viktor Orban's Hungary has been consistently hostile to immigrants since Orban took power, which may of course explain why refugees would give Hungary a wide berth. However, as is the case in Bulgaria – a point which will be referenced again later – the fact that Ukrainians are white Europeans might put a different cast on things.

21 https://www.dailymail.co.uk/news/article-10724673/Russia-loses-eighth-general-34th-colonel-Ukraine-latest-blow-Putins-botched-invasion.html?ito=push-notification&ci=vqkOtd2ryG&cri=zwWycpI4-w&si=43716103&xi=a411470b-4f82-4869-98e9-0161cd935814&ai=10724673

22 https://www.dailymail.co.uk/news/article-10642413/Putins-15th-commander-killed-Ukrainian-forces-say-worst-deaths-brass-WWII.html?ito=push-notification&ci=Lr7OQw_EnR&cri=mitf6ylg72&si=43716103&xi=a411470b-4f82-4869-98e9-0161cd935814&ai=10642413

23 Another Russian general killed in Ukraine (msn.com)

24 Paranoid Putin and his inner circle 'living in top-secret nuke bunkers' sparking fears of nuclear war (thesun.co.uk)

25 Volodymyr Zelensky suggests NATO is 'being run by Russia' as he begs for tanks, planes and anti-ship weapons in Vladimir Putin war | Sky News Australia

26 Declan Walsh, "Slain African Leader Haunts Trial and His Country," The New York Times, Friday, March 11, 2022.

27 See Carlotta Gall, "Mariupol Teetering Amid Signs Russia Is Shifting Focus," New York Times, Monday, March 28, 2022.

28 https://www.msn.com/en-us/news/world/exclusive-zelensky-says-ukraine-won-t-give-up-territory-in-the-east-to-end-war-with-russia/ar-AAWiZ0Q?ocid=entnewsntp&cvid=8753f99c41b-74015804b930a5baa1093 Zelensky must avoid the advice of the likes of Noam Chomsky, who counsels an accommodation with

Putin that would allow the Ukrainian region of Donbas to be granted "autonomy." Chomsky is, in effect, rewarding Russia for its aggression. And, when Chomsky warns against fighting "until the last Ukrainian" he forgets that it is Putin who started this war. Better that we follow Zelensky rather than Chomsky's realpolitik. See Noam Chomsky says Ukraine should settle with Russia (msn.com)

29 In our forthcoming book, Tim Campbell and I name that figure who understands itself as a self that knows what it cannot know the "comic self," also the title of our book. (*The Comic Self,* Minneapolis, University of Minnesota Press, 2023.)

30 When the Australian cricket legend, Shane Warne, passed away in March, 2022, he was lauded for many things. His great gifts as a leg-spin bowler, his pugnacity on the field of play, his ability to "psyche" out opponents. His shortcomings, the drug use, putative or not, the bad boy behavior, the irascibility, too were recalled. However, Warne remained loved. Loved because he never sought to dissemble. He was fully embraced by former team-mates, opponents, the Australian and international cricketing public for one reason above all others: Warne's was an authenticity constituted in no measure as much out of his prodigious talents as out of his all-too human shortcomings. We could speak similarly of other cricketers, Viv Richards, Ian Botham and Freddie Flintoff, not least among them.

31 Declan Walsh, "Slain African Leader Haunts Trial and His Country," *The New York Times,* Friday, March 11, 2022.

32 PAIGC is the Portuguese name: *Partido Africano para a Independência da Guiné e Cabo Verde;* "African Party for the Independence of Guinea and Cape Verde.

33 In the identity politics world that we inhabit, the commitment to instituting equality in its many forms has taken on an unfortunate abbreviation, "DIE" (Diversity, Equity and Inclusion) a fatal – fatalistic – abbreviation which seems to be missed on its advocates. Or, it may be that they prefer to list it as Diversity, Equity and Inclusion – DEI. But that is hardly ideal either. After all, it is Latin for "God." So maybe that's what they want, their critics might say, to play God. That works only to rouse another unwelcome specter – Opus Dei.

34 Zelensky on 'Never Again' vow: 'We don't believe the world' | Watch (msn.com)

35 To be fair, there have also been anti-Russia protests, some of which included diasporic Russians, but they have been, on the whole smaller in size. However, that there is even a pro-Russia sentiment in Serbia is, to say the least, disturbing. https://apnews.com/article/russia-ukraine-vladimir-putin-business-nato-belgrade-ba3d38df4 87cbe9f52a5332bfe55ec6e

36 See Andrew Higgins, "In Serbia, Putin is a 'Brother' and Russia the West's Fellow Victim," *The New York Times*, Thursday, March 31, 2022. As Higgins points out, in Europe a powerful "victim mentality" obtains so that every ethno-nationalism considers itself not only wronged, but legitimate in seeking some form of recognition for its historic injury, some measure of compensation for the costs the injury incurred and, of course, the "injury" it suffered gives it the right to retribution. The only country not to go down this path is Germany.

37 See The $578 million megayacht owned by Russian oligarch Andrey Melnichenko was seized by Italy (msn.com); Putin is made to take evasive action in relation to his yacht "Graceful," Putin's yacht 'Graceful' abruptly leaves Germany amid sanctions warnings over Ukraine (republicworld.com); Putin, it would seem, collects yachts, US intelligence officials believe a $700 million superyacht that's docked in Italy could belong to Russian President Vladimir Putin, reports say (msn.com)

38 Bermuda suspends permits for Russian-operated planes (msn.com)

39 At least 14 private jets from Russia have landed in Israel in the past 10 days amid the latest round of sanctions targeting oligarchs (msn.com)

40 Roman Abramovich's $600 million superyacht was spotted anchored in Montenegro days after the UK imposed sanctions on the oligarch, report says (msn.com)

41 See Matthew Goldstein, "Oligarch Is Squeezed Further with $7 Billion Asset Freeze," *The New York Times Business*, Thursday, April

14, 2022. It would seem that Abramovich's visibility as a Putin ally has made him in some ways more vulnerable to the legal action than some of Putin's other cronies.

42 Where yachts owned by Russian oligarchs are right now - CNN

43 David D. Kirkpatrick, Isabel Kershner, Rory Smith and Tariq Panja, "Putin Oligarch Finds Himself Pariah in West's Playgrounds," *The New York Times*, Saturday, March 12, 2022.

44 "Israel doesn't have a special exemption": Republican slammed for blasting lack of Russia sanctions (msn.com)

45 It turns out, unsurprisingly, that architect of the Bucha atrocities is a "God-fearing' man of the Orthodox variety. https://www.dailymail.co.uk/news/article-10689983/Ukraine-war-Revealed-Butcher-Bucha.html?ito=push-notification&ci=VksnJHTjHl&cri=sSSBzU74Zs&si=43716103&xi=a411470b-4f82-4869-98e9-0161cd935814&ai=10689983

46 Pope Francis' peace prayer for Ukraine recalls prophecy 105 years ago about Russia (ecumenicalnews.com)

47 Pope Francis wrote a letter accusing journalists who speculate that he quietly supports Putin of having a sexual fetish for feces, report says (msn.com)

48 Jason Horowitz, "Pope Denounces Invasion, but Not Mastermind," *The New York Times*, Saturday, March 19, 2022.

49 https://www.bbc.co.uk/religion/religions/christianity/pope/johnpaulii_1.shtml#:~:text=Quite%20early%20on%20John%20Paul,influential%20religious%20order%2C%20the%20Jesuits.

50 Pope Francis washes and kisses feet of Muslim, Hindu and Christian refugees | The Independent | The Independent

51 https://www.msn.com/en-us/news/world/pope-francis-holds-ukrainian-flag-from-martyred-city-of-bucha/vi-AAVUNyu?ocid=entnewsntp&cvid=b6deaec35bec41e59631a003d7877fc5

52 https://www.bbc.com/news/world-europe-60736185

53 Homer, *The Odyssey*, translated by Robert Fagles, New York: Penguin Putnam, 1996, 85.

54 Marikana court case back to haunt Ramaphosa - The Mail & Guardian (mg.co.za)

55 https://www.msn.com/en-us/news/world/s-africa-s-ramaphosa -lashed-on-ukraine-slams-outdated-un-body/ar-AAVXwUP?oc id=entnewsntp&cvid=2d7c71bacdb241b49a19c6aa07df9bdf

56 https://www.msn.com/en-us/news/world/african-support-on-ukraine-shows-kremlin-s-soft-power/ar-AAVTSFE?ocid=entnew sntp&cvid=b6deaec35bec41e59631a003d7877fc5

57 The Olympic champion who turned his back on the Russian regime - and why few in sport will follow - BBC Sport

58 msn.com/en-us/news/world/bjp-s-bulldozer-is-carrying-hatre d-and-terror-congress-leader-rahul-gandhi-slams-mp-govt/ ar-AAW7Onc?ocid=entnewsntp&cvid=d68da7d57cb14effb 216e59b92274484

59 David Byrne, *Bicycle Diaries*, New York: Viking, 2009, 68.

60 UK's PM faces new scrutiny over Russian lord (msn.com)

61 Roman Abramovich: Death and destruction in Ukraine overshadows Russian oligarch's legacy at Chelsea (msn.com)SUI

62 Eddie Howe 'doesn't feel qualified' to speak on Newcastle's Saudi ownership (irishtimes.com)

63 Amnesty International urges Newcastle and Eddie Howe to speak out on Saudi ownership | Football News | Sky Sports

64 Saudi Arabia executes 81 people in show of force by an emboldened Mohammed bin Salman (nbcnews.com)

65 Saudi Arabia executes 81 people in show of force by an emboldened Mohammed bin Salman (nbcnews.com)

66 Saudi Arabia Puts 81 People To Death In Largest Mass Execution | HuffPost Latest News

67 Brittney Griner: Everything we know about the basketball star's detention in Russia (yahoo.com)

68 Granovskaia, Buck 'unlikely to stay' at Chelsea after Abramovich — report - We Ain't Got No History (sbnation.com)

69 Thomas Tuchel 'Uncomfortable' With Situation in Ukraine, 'Hard to Focus' on Football (msn.com)

70 Ukraine conflict: Mariupol theatre hit by Russian air strike had 'children' written on pavement in Russian - satellite images show | The Scotsman

71 Banning the purchasing of Russian coal, a much less lucrative source of revenue for Putin, as the EU did in April, 2022, really is a cop-out. Gas and oil are the major sources of income for Russia. An empty symbolism. When EU members such as Germany rationalize the on-going purchase of Russian oil and gas by saying that sanctions should hurt the Russians more than EU members, they miss the point. Economic calculations should not be the overdetermining factor in imposing sanctions.

72 https://www.dailymail.co.uk/news/article-10619081/Russian-soldiers-say-Putins-d-khead-didnt-want-war.html?ito=push-notification&ci=7hmgk7CqhC&cri=Bae23blOaF&si=43716103&xi=a411470b-4f82-4869-98e9-0161cd935814&ai=10619081

73 https://www.scotsman.com/news/world/russian-journalist-marina-ovsyannikova-why-was-the-russian-journalist-arrested-and-what-was-the-russian-news-protest-3611591

74 See, Michael Schwirtz, "Standing in Russia's Way as the Bodies Pile Up and Life Goes On," The New York Times, March 16, 2022.

75 Then there are those, such as Goldman Sachs CEO David Solomon who, despite having done the right thing by closing down its operation in Russia, seem to be somewhat aggrieved at finding themselves being asked to do right by the Ukrainian people. It's as though Solomon at once wants to be lauded for having done the right thing and also reserves to himself the right to be peeved about having done it. See Goldman Sachs CEO says it's not Wall Street's job to 'ostracize Russia' amid calls on social media for corporations to pull out of the country (msn.com)

76 https://www.nytimes.com/2022/03/16/us/politics/transcript-zelensky-speech.html

77 https://www.dailymail.co.uk/news/article-10736565/Zelensky-launches-social-media-campaign-drum-global-support-arms-

shipments-Ukraine.html?ito=push-notification&ci=TztNCFjHj
r&cri=v49odWTPNL&si=43716103&xi=a411470b-4f82-4869-
98e9-0161cd935814&ai=10736565

78 World's Best Sniper 'Wali' Has Joined Ukrainian Forces Against
Russia. Here's All You Need to Know About Him (news18.com)

79 From devoted nun to ruthless killer: Ukraine claims to have captured Bagira, Russia's most feared and admired sniper (cityam.
com)

80 Winston Churchill Speech – We Shall Fight on The Beaches (pre
sentationmagazine.com)

81 https://www.dailymail.co.uk/news/article-10641677/Meet-fear
some-women-armed-teeth-ready-defend-port-Odessa-seaborn-
invasion.html?ito=push-notification&ci=zYXjqJ5E4I&cri=t2x
cfF4QXd&si=43716103&xi=a411470b-4f82-4869-98e9-
0161cd935814&ai=10641677

See also https://www.dailymail.co.uk/news/article-10654999/Yo
ung-Ukrainian-mothers-tell-taken-arms-defend-Odesa-Putins-
forces.html?ito=push-notification&ci=tCp9Wvx7Xu&cri=xC
LlIz5mPF&si=43716103&xi=a411470b-4f82-4869-98e9-
0161cd935814&ai=10654999

82 Winston Churchill Speech – We Shall Fight on The Beaches (pre-
sentationmagazine.com)

83 A mindset, Meir's Zionism, that has since the inception of the Israeli state done immense violence to the Palestinians. Meir, it is
worth remembering, was brutally dismissive of the Palestinian
cause: "The Palestinians," Meir famously said, "never miss an opportunity to miss an opportunity." Difficult to decide if Meir's dis-
missal is better or worse than Moshe Dayan's insistence that the
Palestinians could "live like dogs" or they "could leave." Zelensky
was hardly treated like a Palestinian dog by the Knesset, but he certainly left his (virtual) meeting with the Knesset empty-handed.

84 Israel Blocked Sale of Pegasus Spyware to Ukraine and Estonia -
The New York Times (nytimes.com)

85 Mark Landler and Marc Santora, "Invoking Churchill, Zelensky
Vows No Surrender," *New York Times*, March 9, 2022.

86 https://www.nytimes.com/2022/03/16/us/politics/transcript-zelensky-speech.html

87 See Steven Erlanger, Eric Schmitt and Julian E. Barnes, *The New York Times*, Wednesday, April 20, 2022. See also As a new, uglier phase of fighting in Ukraine begins, Western countries are rushing to give Kyiv bigger, better weapons (yahoo.com) and Ukraine war: Which countries are sending weapons and aid to forces fighting the Russian invasion? | Euronews

88 Russia-Ukraine: Legacy of Germany's Angela Merkel is seen differently (cnbc.com)

89 Merkel said she stands by her 2008 decision to block Ukraine's NATO bid after Zelenskyy blamed her for war atrocities (msn.com)

90 Ukraine war update, March 24: Zelenskyy calls for global protests against Russia's invasion; Biden travels to Europe (msn.com)

91 https://www.msn.com/en-us/news/world/this-country-is-acc epting-the-most-ukrainian-refugees-according-to-data/ss-AAV Vex0?ocid=entnewsntp&cvid=b6deaec35bec41e59631a003d 7877fc5

92 Etymology of refugee - Search (bing.com) We must keep in mind, as *Webster's* reminds us, to offer refuge is to give protection to, to ensure the safety of those fleeing from danger.

93 https://www.dailymail.co.uk/news/article-10662773/Roman-Abramovich-attends-peace-talks-Turkey-minister-warns-not-eat-drink-meeting.html?ito=push-notification&ci=Bf_49WXAiv&cr i=1MzUgHEz2T&si=43716103&xi=a411470b-4f82-4869-98e9-0161cd935814&ai=10662773

New Titles from
Westphalia Press

Contests of Initiative: Countering China's Gray Zone Strategy in the East and South China Seas
by Dr. Raymond Kuo

China is engaged in a widespread assertion of sovereignty in the South and East China Seas. It employs a "gray zone" strategy: using coercive but sub-conventional military power to drive off challengers and prevent escalation, while simultaneously seizing territory and asserting maritime control.

Frontline Diplomacy: A Memoir of a Foreign Service Officer in the Middle East
by William A. Rugh

In short vignettes, this book describes how American diplomats working in the Middle East dealt with a variety of challenges over the last decades of the 20th century. Each of the vignettes concludes with an insight about diplomatic practice derived from the experience.

Anti-Poverty Measures in America: Scientism and Other Obstacles
Editors, Max J. Skidmore and Biko Koenig

Anti-Poverty Measures in America brings together a remarkable collection of essays dealing with the inhibiting effects of scientism, an over-dependence on scientific methodology that is prevalent in the social sciences, and other obstacles to anti-poverty legislation.

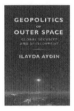

Geopolitics of Outer Space: Global Security and Development
by Ilayda Aydin

A desire for increased security and rapid development is driving nation-states to engage in an intensifying competition for the unique assets of space. This book analyses the Chinese-American space discourse from the lenses of international relations theory, history and political psychology to explore these questions.

Bunker Diplomacy: An Arab-American in the U.S. Foreign Service
by Nabeel Khoury

After twenty-five years in the Foreign Service, Dr. Nabeel A. Khoury retired from the U.S. Department of State in 2013 with the rank of Minister Counselor. In his last overseas posting, Khoury served as deputy chief of mission at the U.S. embassy in Yemen (2004-2007).

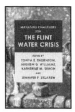

Managing Challenges for the Flint Water Crisis
Edited by Toyna E. Thornton, Andrew D. Williams, Katherine M. Simon, Jennifer F. Sklarew

This edited volume examines several public management and intergovernmental failures, with particular attention on social, political, and financial impacts. Understanding disaster meaning, even causality, is essential to the problem-solving process.

Growing Inequality: Bridging Complex Systems, Population Health, and Health Disparities
Editors: George A. Kaplan, Ana V. Diez Roux, Carl P. Simon, and Sandro Galea

Why is America's health is poorer than the health of other wealthy countries and why health inequities persist despite our efforts? In this book, researchers report on groundbreaking insights to simulate how these determinants come together to produce levels of population health and disparities and test new solutions.

Issues in Maritime Cyber Security
Edited by Dr. Joe DiRenzo III, Dr. Nicole K. Drumhiller, and Dr. Fred S. Roberts

The complexity of making MTS safe from cyber attack is daunting and the need for all stakeholders in both government (at all levels) and private industry to be involved in cyber security is more significant than ever as the use of the MTS continues to grow.

The Politics of Impeachment
Margaret Tseng, Editor

This volume addresses the increased political nature of impeachment. Offering a wide overview of impeachment on the federal and state level, it includes: the politics of bringing impeachment articles forward, the politicized impeachment proceedings, the political nature of how one conducts oneself during the proceedings and the political fallout afterwards.